Let's have a conference!

Let's have a conference!

ELIZABETH LOWRY-CORRY

First published in 1987
© Elizabeth Lowry-Corry, 1987

Published by Aslib, The Association for Information Management
Information House, 26–27 Boswell Street, London WC1N 3JZ
All rights reserved

The illustrations on pages 118–119 are reproduced from the
ACE International Diary by permission of ACE International.

British Library Cataloguing in Publication Data

Lowry-Corry, Elizabeth
  Let's have a conference!
  1. Congresses and conventions
  I. Title
  658.4′562   AS6

  ISBN 0-85142-209-8

Phototypeset in 10/12 point Melliza by Getset (BTS) Ltd,
Eynsham, Oxford
Printed and bound in Great Britain at Page Bros (Norwich) Ltd,
Norwich, Norfolk

Contents

Introduction

'Anyone can organise a conference – it's just a matter of common sense!' Well, yes, but common sense isn't after all so common and there's the matter of doing it well.

Although conference organising is more and more seen as a profession, I see it rather as an art – the art of the possible. Conference literature – the brochures, the manuals, the how-to-do-it articles – is too euphoric; it talks about an ideal situation: speakers you can be sure are good, who can be 'made' to present themselves and their message well; impeccable service, unfailing technology. Whereas in fact you hear 'It puts a great burden on the staff', 'The coffee shop won't be open then', 'The redecoration can't be done this summer'. Not terrible inefficiency or slackness, just real life.

Professional conference organisers will, I hope, pick up a wrinkle here and there and anyway nod their heads in agreement, but this book is really meant for 'anyone'. I hope that, holding it in your hand, you will find that you can organise your conference without too much sweat and tears and will feel strong enough to try a second time.

Good luck!

CHAPTER 1

Walking the course

Let's have a conference! Someone has said it and it is your task to make it happen. Immediately you will be confronted with decisions, tasks, problems, from the content of the programme, recruitment of speakers, date, place, duration, scale, publicity, presentation, costs, about all of which I will talk in detail later. But at this point I think it would be most helpful to describe step by step the process of setting up and producing a conference from the first tentative idea to the departure of the last delegate, you hope to a chorus of appreciative farewells.

'Tell me where is fancy bred, in the heart or in the head?'
The inspiration for a conference can come from many sources: a problem that must be aired, a topic burgeoning with developments and interest, simply an institution's need to put on another show to reassert its identity or keep you busy. You may or may not have much say in this, but the moment a decision in principle has been made to go ahead you should be involved to the hilt. At this initial stage decisions must be taken that are crucial to the success of the conference and you are the one best able to advise on these.

Conference begetters are notoriously over-optimistic. 'They just can't stay away!', 'The exhibition will cover the cost' are common cries; but audiences can and do stay away and costs can defeat you unless they, public and price, are very carefully matched. So during the discussions about object and theme – the keynote speakers who might be approached, the main subject heads and session topics, the daring publicity schemes – it is important to establish such practical details as duration – one, two or three days – residential or non-residential, size, level (not only the intellectual level but the kind of participant and the fee they might be willing to pay), in town, out of town,

1

when. And talking about the time – most things take longer than you expect. A meeting with a sitting-target audience, or on a theme of great immediacy and concern that needs little publicity, can be set up very quickly. Three months is a good working run-up period to an average, fairly uncomplicated one-day event. A big international conference, with the complications of overseas speakers, possibly a call for papers, simultaneous translation, hotel accommodation and a widespread publicity campaign, can take a year or even more. If the whole success of your conference depends on one particular speaker, obviously you must agree a date – preferably a choice of dates – with him or her. Otherwise the more flexibility on this point the better as you start your search for a suitable location. The most attractive venues – be they halls, conference centres or hotels – are generally fairly heavily booked. If you are also having to watch the pennies, this applies still more.

As soon as theme, date and place are established, you can make your first publicity announcement: in the press, in your institution's journal, if you have one, and by making sure your conference is listed in any appropriate listings of conferences or similar events in your field that appear in journals such as *Forthcoming International Scientific and Technical Conferences* (published by Aslib).

Down to the nitty-gritty

Having warned the world of your conference, it is time to set about the practical details of its organisation.

At this point the general ideas about subject and theme must be refined into a coherent programme, with topics and their titles grouped into sessions and names of speakers proposed. Based on this draft programme, you will write your letter of invitation to the speakers, giving them as much information as you can about the scope of the conference in general and, of course, their contribution in particular, and the conditions (i.e. with or without a fee, whether expenses will be met) under which they will participate. At the same time you will be continuing your negotiations with the conference location – obviously you established their charges before booking the accommodation – choosing the menus, discussing the timing of the sessions and catering breaks, double-checking the projection facilities and making quite sure that you have a firm figure for the costs.

Publicity and the programme
The more expeditiously this vital phase of setting up the conference can be completed the better. The programme that you will issue as your main publicity vehicle should ideally be complete, or nearly so. The names of your speakers and the content of their papers, together with any additional goodies like a social programme, visits or an exhibition, are your main selling points. The programme must also, of course, show a fee and carry a form of application to attend. Fixing the fee depends on establishing your budget – always subject to the imponderable of how many people you will actually attract. To do this you need as accurate an estimate as possible of the costs involved – hire of accommodation, catering, projection, printing and publicity, transport if needed, the cost of your speakers in fees, expenses on travel, hotels, their presence at the conference. And don't forget that you and possibly some of your staff will also have to attend the event.

With the issue of the programme your main publicity drive begins and, keeping your eye on the bookings, pressure should be maintained right up until the conference itself. The tendency is for later and later booking, and a second wave of publicity a few weeks before the event is advisable and almost always rewarding.

Documentation – speakers
The issue of the printed programme is also an opportunity to maintain contact with the speakers. You may plan to produce a conference handbook – i.e. an extended programme for those attending, with abstracts of the papers, biographies of the speakers and practical details about the arrangements for the conference. Practical details could include for instance a directional map of the location, information about facilities at the conference centre, a word about publication of the proceedings, if this is planned. A letter to the speakers at this stage can remind and reconfirm the request and conditions in your original invitation and ask for any additional material or information by a certain date. It is also your opportunity to check what

their practical needs – such as projection facilities and hotel accommodation – will be.

Documentation – delegates
Meanwhile, the registrations should be coming in. Acknowledge these with a standard letter and either a receipt for the fee that accompanied the booking or an invoice. On payment of the fee, you may send a ticket of admission to the conference or, as suggested above, you may decide to distribute a handbook to delegates, with any other suitable documentation, shortly before the event.

Documentation for the delegates should go out any time between four weeks and ten days ahead of the conference. This may consist of the simplest of joining instructions or a ticket of admission (if this was not sent as a receipt for the payment of the fee), or it may include the extended programme handbook I mentioned above, tickets or invitations to receptions or visits, details of overnight accommodation if arranged by you, pre-prints of the papers if these are to be issued, and indeed any practical information about the arrangements you think your delegates may need. It may make all the difference to the smooth running of the conference (and the number of last-minute queries you have to handle) if delegates have this information, so it is worth mailing the documentation in good time and allowing for almost inevitable postal delays. This is the moment, too, to contact your speakers again, with the documentation and joining instructions, of course, but also possibly by telephone to reassure yourself that they really are coming and that the arrangements for them and their presentations are in order.

Documentation on this scale suggests a fairly complex event. During the weeks after the issue of the publicity drive and as the bookings come in, you will have been collecting the material – bearing in mind that printing a booklet and reproducing the text of papers take quite some time. Before finally passing your proofs you would have been well advised to revisit the venue, to double-check all the arrangements, from the provision of projection facilities and catering to the location of telephones (and the telephone number for calls to your conference office and the delegates), to the arrangement of the registration area and the exact point of entry for arriving delegates. Do not, however, rely on this visit alone, but confirm all the arrangements in a brief to the location, which should accompany the programme handbook and set out exactly the times of the sessions, the public address and projection needs, the details of catering breaks, bar opening hours and any other special arrangements.

Lists
If this is a residential conference, there will probably be a cut-off date for overnight accommodation held. At this point you can send a list of room bookings to date, subject to revision later, and release or continue to hold – or even increase – your allocation, according to your judgement of what your final number will be. It would also be helpful to your caterer to be given an idea at this stage of what your numbers will be – particularly if they are noticeably different from your original estimate. From your point of view, the later you can give your final figures for both catering and overnight accommodation the better.

Meanwhile, back in your office you will be preparing the name cards for the chairs and speakers for display on the platform, organising badges for delegates, and updating the attendance lists. A flurry of late bookings, of cancellations and changes of plan mean that these lists have to be typed and reproduced at the last possible moment and this, of course, applies to any last-minute changes or additions to the programme itself. At some date agreed with the hotel or conference centre you must give your final figure (on which your account will be based) for catering and overnight accommodation, in the latter case with names.

At the conference
Obviously, as conference organiser you must arrive ahead of the delegates: for a residential conference, especially a large one, I recommend at least twenty-four hours ahead. This will give you time to run through all the arrangements with the host centre, to check the layout of the lecture room and the arrangement of the platform, to unpack your various documents, and to set up your conference office and reception desk. You will need some help with all this. If you can recruit colleagues from your office, so

much the better; they need to be carefully briefed on what is expected of them. You will have named a time for registration to start – inevitably there will be early arrivals, so be ready in good time. The first hours of any conference, large or small, seem hectic. Simultaneously, a large number of people are arriving. They will need to be registered, ticked off on a list, given badges or documentation, directed to the cloakrooms, the sessions, their rooms. At the same time, speakers and chairs will be assembling. They will need to be shown the lecture theatre and to be briefed about the conduct of the sessions. However well prepared you and they have been, there will inevitably be checking of the microphones, adjustment of the projection, rearrangement of the seats or lectern, special requests.

Your foresight and care over the arrangements should see you safely through this critical period and any problems that may arise. Once the conference is under way – the sessions started, the first meal consumed and, best of all, the delegates safely tucked up in bed – you can hope that everything will develop more or less according to schedule. I speak with a slight reservation here, because the vagaries of delegates and the occasional human lapse at the host centre can sabotage the best-laid plans. Never for a moment take your eye off the ball! At the same time you need always to keep slightly *ahead* of events. For instance: there is going to be a reception, so make sure the hosts are in position before the guests arrive; the sessions need to be rapporteured, so pencils and notebooks must be available, and someone on hand to do the reporting; a table plan is needed for the banquet – make sure those on the top table are informed. All the time you need to be anticipating problems and enquiries by displaying notices about what arrangements have been made, what facilities exist.

After so many weeks or months of preparation the end comes very quickly, and suddenly everyone wants to know how to get away. When everyone has left, your own packing and departure seem unimportant after what has gone before. Gather up all your own material and spare documents and anything accidentally left behind by delegates, and do take the time to thank your hosts at the conference centre.

Your tasks after the event can be listed quickly: thanks to all those who have helped, materially or with time, support and co-operation; payment – speakers' expenses, bills from the host centre, hotels, printer and any others (carefully checking the accounts); post mortem. You may have undertaken a formal market-research operation in the form of a questionnaire – more of this later. In any event, a meeting of all those concerned with the inception and production of the conference to consider where you succeeded and where you fell short counteracts the temptation to rest on your laurels – a rest in which no conference organiser dare indulge.

In Appendix 1 you will find a conference calendar summarising this chapter, with a checklist of what to do and when to do it.

CHAPTER 2

The irresistible conference

Is your conference really necessary?
You may think this an improper question when my aim is to
help you to organise a conference – any conference on any
subject – and not to reason why. But if you are conversant and
involved with the content of your conference as well as its
organisation and are to any extent responsible for whether or
not it should occur at all, this is a question you – or any
conference-initiating committee – should ask. For after all, the
surest road to success for any such undertaking is that those you
want to attract feel they simply must attend.

The elusive recipe for success
There is, alas, no sure-fire recipe for this kind of drawing
power. The ability to identify the irresistible topic is a gift, an
art, an entrepreneurial flair, which some lucky people have.
Without it, we must approach the problem more obliquely,
lining up the criteria, the various elements that go to make a
good programme, the hopes and expectations of those we aim to
attract. One proposition I will demolish straight away. It is
sometimes said that the programme really doesn't matter: give
your delegates what they want – to get together in the
pleasantest possible surroundings, with good food, plenty to
drink and the chance to socialise – and your object, the communication and exchange of ideas, is achieved. I don't under-
rate this social aspect, but such an event is simply a house party
rather than a conference in any real sense.

Virtually every area of knowledge can produce some –
perhaps very many – potential themes for a conference, but not
always ones that fit any identifiable audience just when you
want them. Timeliness is of the essence. New knowledge or
developing skills or technologies emerge and people's curiosity

8

is stirred. They want to know about them, they sense their challenges and problems and that they may affect their own work. This, in theory, is the moment to strike. But if you have misjudged this interest and it is still in fact only academic, if the practical implications are not yet applicable in the real world and the threat, if any, is something that can be conveniently ignored, you may find that your forward-looking topic is ahead of its time and lacking in drawing power. An example of this can be seen in the progress of computer-aided translation as a conference theme, which as I write seems to be a hot favourite and a powerful draw. The first conferences on the subject, years ago, seemed to suggest that machine-aided translation was still a long way off and could perhaps never be. The translators themselves hated the idea and were glad to stay away. Only in 1978 did the technology reach the point when its application and the issues this raised had to be faced. Since then the developments have been so rapid and the experience of their use so interesting that attendances at conferences on translating and computers have steadily grown. Now, of course, a bandwagon is developing, everyone wants to exploit an 'in' subject and, as the conference organiser looks for new developments and nuances in a popular theme and new sections of the public to attract, the danger of clashes and overlaps – if not downright overkill – grows.

What does the audience want?
Another approach is to look at your audience. What are their needs, expectations, hopes? Well, knowledge, of course, how to make money, avoid tax, how to keep ahead, survive. As well as learning, they need to express their own ideas or air their particular problems, test them against the opinions and experience of others and out of the exchange and clash arrive at new perspectives or solutions. Less overtly, perhaps, as well as airing and promoting ideas, they seek to promote themselves, some cause close to their hearts, or some service, product or expertise they can offer. For people working in the same area of interest a conference can provide a great sense of solidarity, sympathy, support, and stimulation, and a means of keeping up with developments and keeping in touch. The annual conference of an organisation, with its elements of a tribal gathering, is the prime example of this aspect of conference-going, and the

actual structure of the event – something very much in the organiser's hands – plays a great part in this. Finally, if you are launching a very new subject, I would recommend some sort of market research, on a formal or informal basis, although I often think that interpreting your findings is as difficult and inconclusive as the research itself.

Hunt the theme . . .
The most fertile breeding-ground for conference ideas is a highly intelligent and articulate community concerned with broadly the same area of interest but seeing it from widely different points of view. If you are a member of that community you start with an inbuilt advantage, and if you have a committee of such people you are lucky indeed. It is with such a committee, having decided on the overall theme of your conference, that I visualise you starting to plan your programme. (But as I am pledged to talking about conference organising as it is and not as one would wish it to be, I must mention here that sometimes the most brilliant committee produces no ideas at all and every attempt at 'brainstorming' meetings falls flat. I weep for you as I have so often wept for myself and can only say that the journals, the press, TV, contacts, contacts, contacts – just anyone you can talk to, your own imagination and persistence must be your main resource. And I wish you the best of luck!)

You now have to decide on the broad subject headings under which you will deal with your theme, the main speakers or at any rate the kinds of speakers, and how you will find them. A lively committee may easily fight its way through all the issues of the conference while you frantically take notes and anxiously wonder what you have to go on in the way of concrete suggestions to follow up. But take heart, the fact that so much discussion is sparked off probably means you are on to something good and controversial, and you must prepare yourself to pursue the ideas thrown out with research of your own. The packaging of your theme – and that means the physical shape of your programme and its duration – determines how it works in presenting ideas and as a forum for all the other modes of communication, formal and informal, that I have described as part of the package your audience wants, and this very important decision must also be made at this initial stage.

. . . and give it form

Simplest of all is the plenary session – suitable for the presentation of formal papers to an audience of almost any size. When you are planning this remember to allow enough time. Don't overcrowd your papers; brief your speakers very firmly on how long they have to speak and don't allow them to overrun. Leave plenty of time for catering breaks – this kind of generosity eases the timekeeping a little. If you want to encourage audience participation, allow definite and ample periods for discussion.

'More discussion' is a persistent cry in comments on conferences, and with a single-session format it can be quite difficult to stage-manage. A really small gathering presents no problems. The room can, perhaps, be arranged informally – schoolroom style (chairs at desks), in a U or semicircle at a table, or casually round the room. With small numbers the shy are probably not inhibited from taking part and a good chair should be able to stimulate questions when an audience is temporarily dumbfounded, or prevent the garrulous or combative from getting out of control. For a large audience and formal arrangement, one device is the so-called 'panel discussion'. For this all the speakers in a session are gathered on the platform and with some prompting from the chair (or possibly advance briefing from you) generate a discussion, in which diverse views – preferably – are aired and in which members of the audience may be moved to take part.

An interesting format suggested to me once would be particularly suitable for a conference with the definite intention of airing opposing views and arriving at a consensus or some kind of concrete statement or conclusion. Delegates were seated at tables of eight or ten, at which the various factions were equally represented. After a general statement from the platform, each table would discuss among themselves – and with such small numbers this could be an uninhibited exchange of ideas – and produce their united comments or questions, possibly in writing, to be dealt with from the platform. Further variety could be produced by 'shuffling' the delegates and moving them to different tables, only ensuring that the balance between the different interest groups was maintained.

Attention and the audience

Holding the interest should be a prime object of your programme planning. It is difficult to listen uninterruptedly –
hence the need for coffee breaks and question sessions – and
the weight and level of your discourses need to be varied –
hence the device of the so-called 'keynote paper', which aims to
open up the topic, set it in its general perspective, suggest the
main lines of interest. For this paper you will seek your most
prestigious speaker. You may perhaps follow this with two or
three shorter, more informal papers, dealing in depth with some
of the detailed issues involved and looking from a personal
rather than a global view. I will add here (though I will come to
this in more detail in a later chapter) that nothing holds attention better than good and varied presentation – a lively
delivery, the touch of wit, and good and relevant visual aids,
such as slides, diagrams and film.

Participation and diversification

To return to audience participation and its close relative, diver-
sification. One answer to this is multiple or parallel sessions, so
much in demand, so bitterly criticised. Of course, some conferences, such as the British Association for the Advancement of
Science's great annual meetings (which are still going after
more than 150 years), are built on the concept of parallel
sessions – sixteen or more programmes proceeding simultaneously, with only one or two occasions when the whole
conference is all together, and a limited number of occasions
when two or more sections, with their different disciplines,
unite in joint sessions. This suits the great diversity of interests
embraced by the British Association – though I dare say they
have the odd complaint about clashes too – but in a more
homogeneous subject the choices offered sometimes seem to
tantalise more than they please. But parallel sessions do
undoubtedly add to the depth, interest and scope of a programme and, if only for the practical considerations of accom-
modating them and finding and paying for their speakers, it is
essential to know if they are to take place right from the start.
The same, of course, applies to the working party or study
group, for which quite a considerable number of small rooms

may be needed, all to be taken into account when you decide on your location and work out your budget.

'Choose good speakers'

Speakers ('Choose good ones' is the most frequent and all-too-obvious advice offered) are the stars of your show. They are as important – some would say more important – than the theme itself. But unlike the impresarios of stage and screen, you cannot pick them from a queue of eager applicants, nor can you audition their performance and turn the inadequate away. Your speakers are not actors, orators or TV personalities, but professional people, immersed in their speciality and in many cases doing you a favour by speaking at all. Eloquence is for them – and you – an added bonus, and it must be confessed that some of the greatest experts are without it. So, what are you looking for? Well, content of course, real mastery of the subject and, if possible, a new and original view of it; at a very basic level, audibility and a good delivery (and if you are inviting speakers whose mother tongue is not English, be very careful to check on this); a well constructed paper covering the ground without becoming bogged down in irrelevancies, arriving at some kind of point or conclusion, and limited to the allotted time. Audiences often complain when papers are read. I think this is a little unreasonable, and there are devices – which I will describe in a later chapter – to get round this, but a really good paper given without a text and apparently without a note by an expert and enthusiastic speaker can have a liveliness and spontaneity that is particularly appealing.

How to find these paragons? From your personal experience or that of the members of your committee, from hearsay, reputation. A few thoughts that it may be helpful at least to bear in mind. Academics are accustomed to lecturing to classes, which means they have some experience of speaking in public. Members of large consultancies have probably made it their business to present themselves and their subjects well. The author of a well-written book clearly knows how to use words though he or she may not be so fascinating face to face. Politicians of all kinds can generally make speeches but often find it difficult to do more than utter platitudes. Although there are various ways in which you can help your speakers – with suggestions about presentation and visual aids, and of course a very clear description of what you want them to say and for how long, the overall theme and object of the conference, and how their contribution fits into this and with the contributions of the other speakers – you have very little control over what they produce on the day. This applies even when you are paying a fee and far more, of course, when (as so often with institutional conferences) no fee is being paid.

The call for papers
Many conferences build their programmes on a call for papers, relying on this completely or as an adjunct to just a very few keynote papers for which speakers are invited. This can be an economy, as fees are not paid for papers so submitted, although you would probably have to pay such speakers' expenses at the conference and perhaps their travel as well. This approach is particularly suitable for a well-established research conference, at which people in the forefront of their subject are eager to present their latest findings. With less reputation and prestige you can find that few and not very distinguished papers are all you get. To deal with submitted papers received in response to a call, you need a very well qualified and hard-working committee of referees and a readiness to reject the second-rate. It is also worth remembering that you must allow plenty of time – several weeks for a response to the call (which will mostly arrive after the closing date) and a few more weeks to study the papers and construct your programme. You will meet here also – more than when you are inviting your speakers – the risk that the authors of your chosen papers may not present them particularly well.

It is in this kind of programme, with perhaps a very large number of submitted papers which you would like to include, that the device of the preprint can come into its own. The chosen speakers will be asked to provide the texts of their papers in sufficient time for them to be reproduced and distributed to delegates in advance of the conference – or possibly as a proceedings volume which is given to delegates on arrival. The authors are then only expected to introduce their papers quite briefly and the rest of the allotted time can be spent in questions and discussion, the audience having already acquainted themselves with the content of the paper. The device of asking an invited speaker for a text for preprinting or publishing that he will not read but to which he will make a more informal presentation often seems a way of avoiding the read paper, but it does mean more work for the speaker and you must use your own judgement whether you can ask for this extra effort.

A total view

I want to conclude this chapter about the most important phase of your conference planning – the establishment of the theme, format, programme, and speakers – by pulling the threads together in a thoroughly down-to-earth way. You need to act on all these decisions more or less at once and as quickly as possible. And concurrently, and largely dependent on them, a great many more decisions will have to be made. The location of your conference (which I will talk about next) should be chosen as soon as the physical shape – date, size, scope, and financial level – is agreed. Your speakers' invitations or call for papers can follow the moment these decisions have been made. Only when the location is settled and the speakers are secured can you prepare a realistic budget, and the details of the speakers and topics (as well as the price) are the stuff of your publicity drive. So you see how closely these early stages of planning interlock and how vital, from the start, an overall view is to the venture's success.

CHAPTER 3

Accommodation – what and where?

'Look before you leap'

Never pick any location without seeing it first and, even when you are being wooed with drinks or lunch or a well-orchestrated facilities visit (not that I'm against such blandishments), keep your eyes skinned and senses alert. Do you smell the lunch in the auditorium (or hear the washing up)? Does the operation of the lift make the image projected on the screen flicker? Are the auditorium, reception and/or exhibition and catering areas really close to each other? How near are the telephones and the toilets? Metaphorically, if not actually, feel the beds.

Embarras de richesse

You are faced with a bewildering choice of locations, described in the most mouthwatering terms. If you are in the incentive conference business, you may feel able to look for châteaux in France, palazzi in Italy; you might even like the call of the wild to penetrate your conference and go to Kenya where 'special touches can include champagne breakfasts and gala dinners . . . as coffee and liqueurs are served round the camp fire, Masai warriors will emerge from the bush dancing and chanting their war songs'. Well, although standards for even the most basic accommodation are rising all the time, one can manage with a good deal less than that.

Where, tell me where?

How do you know where to look? In Appendix 2 you will find a list of useful addresses which includes some sources of information about meeting and conference accommodation. Hotels advertise, and once you or your organisation is known as a conference producer brochures will arrive. If you are a member of ACE International (the Association of Conference Executives) you will receive their journal *Conference World* and, as a bonus, Spectrum Communications Group's *The Conference Blue Book*, which lists all UK hotels offering conference facilities. Local tourist offices will advise about facilities and so will national tourist offices if you are looking overseas. Finally, there is the network of personal recommendations and advice.

Good plain fare – quality without frills
Let's start with the simplest form of event – the one-day conference – and at the bottom end of the market. Your basic requirements here are a lecture hall that will take the maximum size of audience expected to attend; a foyer for the reception and registration of delegates, adjoining which should be a cloakroom and a sufficiency of toilets; a place and facilities for catering. The variations on this basic theme are enormous but at least you should demand pleasant conditions, comfortable seating, good acoustics, ventilation and lighting (and blackout if you're showing slides), and an adequate platform for speakers.

In checking these points, look at the height of the room: if it is lower than eight feet you may need mechanical ventilation (noiseless, please!). Heating – neither too hot nor too cold – should be adjustable. Electricity: at least one – preferably more – three-pin socket, at either end of the room. Doors and windows that when closed exclude external noise, and doors that don't creak. In larger rooms for more ambitious events these requirements are simply multiplied: more electric points judiciously distributed about the room (and if electrically powered equipment is being used a fire extinguisher should be available). Lighting should be controlled within the room and there should be at least two (or whatever is laid down by the local fire authority) unlocked and marked exits for the duration of the meeting. A raised platform for the speakers, always desirable, becomes a necessity as your numbers approach the hundred mark. Good projection and public address systems are also essential, as is a telephone. Ideally, the location should provide these – bringing in equipment is far less satisfactory – and, in any case, pin boards, blackboard, screen and lectern, and such accessories as drawing pins, adhesive tape, chalk, blackboard eraser, ashtrays, water jugs, and glasses should be available automatically. (They aren't always, so it is worth checking.)

The condition and size of the adjoining foyer are also important. You will need to set up a table at which two or more people can be seated with space to lay out badges, attendance lists, spare programmes, and other documents. There must be room for perhaps the majority of conference delegates to register more or less simultaneously without unseemly crush. Ideally, this foyer should be the area where all the delegates can foregather in reasonable comfort and where, between sessions, tea or coffee can be served. A pay bar and telephone in this area would be an added bonus. In a really large foyer it might be possible to serve a buffet lunch; if not, an adjoining room to accommodate your catering will have to be available. Catering at the back of a large lecture hall, though I've seen it done, is not satisfactory, for the obvious reasons of the clatter of plates and the post-prandial mess. However, one does sometimes have to accept conditions that are less than ideal.

Catering is obviously a prime consideration and often one gets the impression that what people remember about conferences is the lunch – certainly you hear about it if it's not good! Sometimes those providing the conference accommodation can do the catering and if so you may find that the hire of the hall is calculated per capita on the number of delegates and depends largely on the cost of the lunch. Alternatively, your location may have certain 'tied' or recommended caterers, to which they direct you, or you may be allowed to employ an outside caterer of your own choice. In the latter case, it is wise to put the caterers in touch with the location, so that they are familiar with the conditions under which they will be working.

There is a very wide range of this kind of accommodation and it would be impossible as well as invidious to name names, so I will just talk a little about broad types available. Many institutions have a room with adjoining facilities that are adequate for small events. Others – such as Aslib – are lucky enough to have a custom-built lecture theatre and some or all of the supporting services. Universities and polytechnics have – and some offer – lecture rooms, some of which are available all the year round, others during school or university holidays only. Some provide conference accommodation on a serious and regular basis, with catering and supporting facilities included. Accommodation of this nature is generally very modestly priced, but it is worth bearing in mind that providing conference accommodation and services is ancillary to the main function of such institutions, whose first duty is to their members or students, and is often undertaken by people whose main task is very different and who may find it difficult to give your demands the priority they need. You have to be alert for such attitudes and can only assess them in personal contact – not a very easy judgement to make.

Step up-market
Once you are able to move up-market a little, the choice lies between custom-built conference centres – such as the Central Electricity Generating Board's Sudbury House, the London Press Centre, the Brewery (Whitbread's conference centre), the Confederation of British Industry's conference suite at Centrepoint, the Institute of Marine Engineers, Wembley, the Barbican, the New Westminster Centre – and hotels. Here also quality and price vary widely, and both centres and hotels, when they have a good reputation and are not exorbitantly expensive, are pretty heavily booked.

I have to admit a personal preference for conference centres, where the halls are custom-built, generally with excellent, varied projection and public address facilities and trained technicians to operate them, and where the needs of the presentation come first. Such establishments almost always provide catering, either from their own kitchens or using a 'tied' outside caterer. Sometimes, like most hotels, they offer a conference 'package', so much per delegate, which includes all catering and room hire, and sometimes, but not always, projection. Others have a hire charge for the rooms and a per-head charge for catering according to whatever scale of menu you choose.

I have noticed that a lot of delegates are partial to hotel accommodation and I agree that when it is good it is very pleasant, but there are perhaps more pitfalls for you in making this choice: the auditorium has not been custom-built and so may not be so good – and certainly won't be raked; projection arrangements may be far more haphazard; you may 'lose' your delegates to other parts of the hotel; the catering may be obtrusive and take too long. Prices, like for like, are fairly comparable, so it is very much a matter of which best suits your individual needs and preferences and is available on the required day.

The residential conference

If you are embarking on a conference of two days or longer, you will have had to decide whether to make it wholly or in part residential. Various factors will have governed this decision, not least what you think will please your particular audience. Undoubtedly, to bring all your delegates under one roof and to keep them there creates a total experience that no other formula provides. This is particularly suited to a medium-sized conference – say under 100 – where there is great identity of interest or where it is intended that some kind of decision or initiative should emerge from the discussion. These numbers, too, can reasonably be accommodated under one roof – say in a medium-sized hotel, an Oxford or Cambridge college, or one of the custom-built conference centres (some of them converted stately homes), mostly in the country, that offer residential conference accommodation. When it comes to a larger conference, say 200 or more, your choice lies between a university or a really large and probably several-star hotel. In either case, the attraction of the place itself, the beauty or interest of the neighbourhood, will probably weigh in your choice.

Glades of Academe

A university's most obvious advantage over hotel accommodation is price. Many modern universities, with their halls of residence and often centralised catering, can accommodate numbers of the order of 250 – 400 more or less together. Some of the campuses are built outside the towns where they are

located, creating a self-contained unit and thus for your conference a kind of 'togetherness' ('togetherness in discomfort' I can
hear some of you murmur), which you may want to establish
and which many participants like. The university's other area of
excellence is in the accommodation for the sessions themselves.
Generally you will find more and better theatres, raked or
otherwise, of various sizes, and seminar rooms for workshops;
the public address and projection facilities, with trained operators, are often of a high standard and not highly priced.

It is obviously more difficult and challenging to run a good
conference on a tight budget and as university accommodation
is one of the answers to this, I think it is worth looking at it very
closely. Although you will not find private bathrooms, colour
TV or telephones in university single study-bedrooms (sorry,
very few doubles), the accommodation can be perfectly adequate in a modest way; in many universities, the beauty of the
setting, the excellence of lecture facilities (and, one hopes, the
programme), the feel and atmosphere of the place, as well as the
reasonable price, compensate for this. The quality and range of
facilities vary widely and need to be assessed very carefully to
arrive at the most satisfactory mix. What do not vary too much
are the prices charged, so that having decided on this type of
accommodation, you should not have to take the cost factor too
much into account.

A further similarity is likely to be in the way your reservation
and financial arrangements are handled; they will be with the
university direct – no extra bills run up by delegates, no
individual booking. You will provisionally reserve the number
of rooms you expect to need and at a date nearer the conference
confirm this figure, at which point there will be some financial
penalty if you fall below your 'guesstimate'. The university will
give you a figure for full board per head per day – which can
however be broken down for those taking meals only – and the
handling of the room reservations (and sometimes the allocation of the rooms) will fall entirely on you. This is a heavy
workload, but your aim will be to offer the conference as a total
package – the programme of sessions, attendance at exhibition
(if there is one), social and any other activities – plus full board
and lodging, for a comprehensive fee. Although you can never
avoid some part-timers and demands for variations on the basic

offer, this does simplify the room booking procedure and, by making it significantly cheaper to buy the package as a whole rather than piecemeal, you may encourage your delegates to stay for the duration of the conference.

Nowhere, particularly at a budget price, can you find everything you want. Here are some of the conditions you should demand: a good standard of bedroom (washbasin with hot and cold water in all of them is, in my view, a must; a point for razors and a bedside light are highly desirable, and here you should actually feel the beds!); bathrooms in preference to showers, and the bathroom area not open-plan; spacious and pleasant lounges and sufficient bars; a high standard of lecture hall or halls and good projection facilities; good catering. The demand for compactness grows. Delegates hate walking – and some really can't – and the weather can be a dampener in a literal sense. Although bussing from hall of residence to meals or sessions is possible, it is an added complication and expense, and taxing for the delegates themselves. Even more important than the closeness of the residences to the sessions and catering is the compactness of this 'action area' itself. Ideally, the lecture hall or halls should immediately adjoin the area where midsession tea and coffee is served, be near the bar or bars and also near the dining hall. There is at present a great vogue for exhibitions to support and illustrate conferences; this opens up a whole new vista of possibilities and problems but from the accommodation point of view it means that you must have a large area very close to the sessions, catering and bars, an area that delegates simply can't help frequenting. To build your exhibition, this area must be provided with power cables and points (or it must be possible to install them) and the university administration must be able and willing to cope with this. Catering – so important a contribution to delegates' contentment – is not easy to assess as you probably won't have a chance to sample what is actually served to delegates, and has to some extent to be taken on trust. Spend as much on it as your budget will allow; look for a dining room that can seat the whole conference at once (you may be planning a banquet); for routine streamlining of self-service to minimise queues or for waitress service (which everyone prefers but I fear is on the way out).

While you are looking at all this, take note of where – or whether – there is parking space, if there are telephones, how easy it is to find your way about the area, if there is a shop, a bank, a post office, above all, what the conference management and staff are like.

Which university?
As you study universities for conferences you will notice their assets and disadvantages, weighing them against each other. There is, for instance, an initial prejudice in favour of Oxbridge. Dining in those stately college halls (and their cellars are often rather good), the sheer beauty and atmosphere of the place and its surroundings may compensate for having to walk a little way down streets that are not suitable for bussing to the sessions and exhibition (but not, I suggest, for bathrooms across the quad!). Oddly enough, Oxford and Cambridge are not well provided with lecture accommodation. If your numbers exceed what can be fitted into some of the newer colleges – such as Churchill or Wolfson in Cambridge or St Catherine's in Oxford, which have their own lecture theatres – you will have to use departmental lecture theatres, which may not be very close. Parking in either of these wonderful cities is a nightmare.

The newer universities show varying standards of building and design (depending largely on government lavishness or otherwise at the time of their erection) and very different standards of maintenance and use. Some take the whole conference operation very seriously and bend over backwards to make their accommodation fit this purpose as well as the students' needs. In others you detect a certain 'take it or leave it' attitude. The ability and dedication of the conference manager (whatever title is used can be revealing) and the clout he or she carries in the rest of the university is vital to your assessment of the feel of the place and your sense that the total package will work. And however good the package, there will be snags. The weak link often proves to be service – just not enough, unimaginative or inflexible. This is not a harsh judgement but a simple recognition that you get what you pay for, and you find it also in hotels, despite the 'Ask your friendly hotel manager' in the advertisements.

Option hotel

If you have decided on a hotel for your conference, you are committed to a much more expensive operation and you will need to be very sure you're getting value for money. You will need to check the lecture and projection facilities with special care. Ideally, these will have been built for the purpose; if not, make sure the ballroom does really convert well; that there is blackout, good ventilation, and a public address system; and that the hotel can cope with all your projection needs. As in a university, the exhibition, if you have one, must be placed where it is under the eyes of the delegates, there must be access for the exhibits, and the possibility of installing power cables, points and telephones. Catering for your delegates should be separate from the other residents – assuming you have not taken over the whole hotel – and so should the bar and lounge. Look into possibilities for a banquet, dinner dance or disco. All this, at the standard you want, is likely to mean an up-market hotel with a fairly high room rate. Your speakers and important guests for whom you have to pay will be accommodated here and, if making this a residential conference is essential to your whole concept of the project, it is important to be confident that the great majority of your audience will be willing to pay the hotel price. You should, of course, be able to negotiate a special rate below the hotel's normal level and in some cases the hire charge for the lecture halls may be reduced or waived if you take up enough bedrooms. Room bookings should be directed to the hotel, which should handle them and bill the delegates individually. If you are not able to make this arrangement with the manager, I would have the greatest reservations about using the hotel.

Back to basics – where?

At this point I'd like to go back to one of the first decisions you'll have to make about the location of your conference: where – in the sense of London or the provinces, town or country, or abroad? Obviously this is dictated by circumstances. If you are a London-based institution seeking to attract an audience in the metropolitan area and the south-east, London would seem to be the obvious choice. If you are based in the midlands, the south-west, or in Scotland, the same local arguments of accessibility for your audience apply. A short, quick journey is important. So, too, are good communications – by rail, road and, if necessary, by air. Even for the 'get away from it all' conference, this is important (unless you provide transport); too long a journey should be avoided (and here expense comes into the picture). Where you go is also dictated by the kind of accommodation you need. If you have decided on a non-residential conference, you must choose a location which most of your delegates can reach travelling each day from home and where hotel accommodation can be found for those from further afield. Your choice of a conference centre in the country for a small to medium-sized residential conference may be influenced not only by its accessibility but the attraction of the setting as well as its suitability for your event. In discriminating between universities there will be other considerations besides the accommodation itself. Is this a city or neighbourhood that will attract delegates in its own right? Has it features that are of interest to your particular audience – would a programme of local visits be a rewarding feature of your programme? Is there a generous and welcoming attitude to conferences – for instance, might a civic reception be offered? The larger your conference the narrower your choice, for you will have to find a large enough conference centre with all the attendant facilities and enough hotel accommodation with as wide as possible a price range. For an international conference, you will again need to think of air communications, but, more than this, I believe the drawing power of the place itself is a prime con- sideration: the prestige of a capital city and all that it can offer; a centre of special concern to the topic of your conference; a place with some special claim to fame – beauty, history, excellence in learning or the arts; the more mundane but equally sought- after delights of a tourist centre – good shops and restaurants, facilities for entertainment and so forth.

Overseas
Taking your conference abroad is quite an undertaking and your motives for doing so should be weighed with care. Here I think the glamour of the place is at a premium and for incentive conferences this is undoubtedly the most popular answer for the delegates themselves. A more or less calculable number of

bodies that can be moved *en masse* will make you eligible for a hotel and travel package that could be financially very favourable and enable you to forecast pretty accurately what the venture will cost. For a conference which you have to sell, where your delegates decide independently to attend and you cannot be certain what your numbers will be, the charm of 'abroad' may not compensate for the inevitable higher cost to the delegates and greater risk and effort for you. The real justification for an overseas conference is that it is aimed primarily at a public for whom the particular place is a convenient focal point – a site on the continent of Europe if you are looking for EEC delegates, for instance; in Kenya if you are addressing yourself to the developing world. Like Paris, Brussels and Berlin, London itself is a great attraction and one of the leading conference cities in the world. Nevertheless, my experience of the EURIM (European Conference on Research into the Management of Information Services and Libraries) series did show that the strongest support came from the 'locals', and in hard times competitive price and minimal travel costs make it much easier for your public to attend.

For example . . .
There are many possible formats for your conference – hotel, university, conference centre-based; residential, non-residential, a mix. It is the mix that makes for complications in costing, effort and fee. Let us consider two typical scenarios and see how their problems might be met.

1. Four days, 700 – 1,000 delegates, UK
The programme for this conference demanded plenary sessions on Days 1 and 4 and broke into four parallel sessions on Days 2 and 3. It was planned as a whole, with delegates staying for the full four days (although in the event a small minority attended for individual days only) and, as the catchment area for the audience was the whole of the United Kingdom with a sprinkling from overseas, residential accommodation was needed for the great majority of delegates. Well served by road and rail, B——was chosen for this event because the custom-built conference centre (which provided the necessary large auditorium and smaller halls for the parallel sessions as well as space for a

small exhibition) was within five miles of the university campus where about half the delegates stayed. They were accommodated on a bed, breakfast and dinner basis, and buses brought them to the centre in the morning and returned them to the university in time for the evening meal. Speakers, guests and senior members of the organisation were accommodated in a hotel near the conference centre, where a block booking was made and a special rate negotiated. The rest of the hotel bookings were handled by a hotel booking service, to which delegates were asked to apply direct. The conference complex offered bars and catering facilities of a cafeteria kind, while some delegates found their way to bars and restaurants nearby or returned to their hotels for lunch. Between-session teas and coffees were served in the conference centre, in the foyers outside the auditorium and meeting rooms. It was particularly fortunate that the complex's own catering and the local facilities were able to take care of lunch for such a large number, as making special arrangements would have increased both the financial commitment and the administrative load for the organisation.

This conference was aimed at a wide range – financially speaking – of delegates and it was important to keep the basic cost of attending as modest as possible (hence the opportunity to opt for university accommodation, and the hotel booking service was specifically asked to offer some budget-priced hotels). It was decided therefore to charge a basic fee which included attendance at all the sessions and the exhibition, the 'welcome' reception, the reception offered by the city, and the mid-session teas and coffees. To encourage attendance for the whole conference, the per-day rate offered was rather more than a quarter of this fee. Lunches and hotel accommodation were at the delegates' own expense. The charge for university accommodation was made on a daily bed, breakfast and dinner rate and included the cost of any bus transport to and from the university. This charge was shown as a separate item from the conference fee when invoicing. Because it was envisaged that all delegates would not be staying the full four nights, the idea of a composite fee for attendance and accommodation in the university was rejected. The conference banquet was an optional extra and charged as such on the invoices. An official travel agent was not appointed for this event, but on booking all delegates were given forms of application for the concessionary rail fares offered by British Rail to conference delegates.

2. Three days, 300 delegates, overseas

An overseas location is, in my view, really only justified if a truly international audience can be guaranteed. Obviously, the city and country should be chosen for its accessibility to the greatest number of potential delegates and if a high proportion of these can come from the host country, so much the better. For a 300-strong, three-day conference, a centre in Holland provided these conditions, with simultaneous translation facilities permanently *in situ* and a recommended firm of interpreters, with whom it was necessary to deal direct. There were a number of medium- to top-grade hotels near the conference complex and the hotel bookings were handled by the centre, to which delegates were asked to apply. The only snag that arose with this excellent arrangement was that the deposit asked for by the hotels on making a reservation was sometimes delayed, owing to the dilatoriness of the international banking system, giving rise to a last-minute flurry about unconfirmed bookings. This is something that clearly need not happen but perhaps should be borne in mind if such a condition is demanded by the hotels. For those delegates travelling from the United Kingdom, it was possible to negotiate a package, travelling on a choice of two flights out and back to London; this included transport from the airport to hotels in the vicinity of the centre and back to the airport at the end of the conference. The programme of the conference was homogeneous and closely packed and all catering – mid-session breaks and lunches – was on site, using a caterer recommended by the centre.

Catering is, of course, a costly item and you must try to arrive at a figure for the caterer which is as nearly accurate as possible, thereby avoiding many uneaten meals or the embarrassment of not having provided enough. Overseas conferences, to an exceptional degree, seem to attract registrations – made at the last minute by telephone or telex and not paid for in advance – that do not materialise or are only paid for on arrival, and at the same time an incalculable number of bookings on the day, from people who still expect to be fed. A tempting solution would be to insist on advance payment for all registrations, but I think this would be difficult to enforce and such rigidity might reduce your attendance to a regrettable extent. The fee for this particular conference was, of course, non-residential, but otherwise all-inclusive, and a per-day rate was not quoted.

Using a conference centre in the heart of a city that enjoys a reputation for eating out and where restaurants of varying grades abound, you may decide to leave delegates to make their own arrangements for lunch. The continent does not seem to share the British passion for mid-morning coffee and tea, and delegates at international conferences often seem to prefer to slip away between sessions to buy a coffee or a drink at the bar that is almost always provided in the centre. With such arrangements, of course, you would charge a fee that simply covered attendance at the conference itself and any social aspects of the programme, such as visits or a reception, for which the conference budget had to pay. For any non-residential conference overseas it is essential to employ a reliable agency to handle hotel bookings. In many German cities, the Tourist Office (Fremdensverkehrsamt) offers a highly efficient service and the same can be said for many of the Syndicats d'Initiative in France. Alternatively, you can approach a travel agent or a hotel booking service in the city where your conference will be held (and here the advice of the conference centre itself or any local member of your committee would be invaluable). Concurrently, if a considerable number of delegates are coming from this country, I would recommend using a travel agency located here and negotiating with them a hotel and travel package.

A residential conference overseas involves using a hotel or a conference centre that can provide overnight accommodation. It represents a large financial commitment for the organiser and is likely to be costly in terms of fee – particularly if you are planning a large conference (despite the economies of scale that size can bring), as only high-class hotels are likely to have the necessary facilities. However, even the best hotels do have low seasons and in such a case it would be well worth approaching a reputable travel agent to see what sort of a package they could negotiate for you, remembering that package travel means fixed times and places of departure for travellers and a fixed duration of stay. It would also be very important to inspect personally any hotel offered and to read any small print very carefully before concluding the deal.

Packages

Packages, deals – in some ways these lead on to my next chapter, which is concerned with finance. This is the age of the package, largely because standardisation reduces administrative effort and so cost. Look for this kind of standardisation in your accommodation and travel arrangements and adhere to it as far as you can. Don't try to handle any travel package or concession you've been able to arrange yourself. Tell your delegates about it, show them how to apply, and leave it up to them. Delegates on the whole are not themselves susceptible to standardisation; at the same time, too many options offered by you are confusing, lead to too many variations of the fee, and lead to questions and argument. The answer as I see it, therefore, is a mix, such as a composite fee including full residence, or a basic fee plus the offer of an optional travel and hotel package (particularly overseas), or the opportunity to make their own choice of hotel, either independently or through a recommended service. Your object must be to make booking for your conference as easy and convenient as possible for your delegates without taking on the task of travel agent and hotel reception on top of your own – in short, to obtain the best of both worlds for yourself and your clients.

Taking the plunge – the reservation

This survey of accommodation in all its permutations is leading you to a decision – to make a booking. This booking, be it for an afternoon in a college lecture theatre or a week in a Sheraton International, must be confirmed in writing, setting out what you have bespoken and the cost in unequivocal terms. There is an established ritual for this booking process. First, the inspection visit: your examination (and inward assessment) of the accommodation, with perhaps the date 'pencilled in', but with no commitment on either side. Next, the provisional booking. You may still be uncertain of the date or of your committee's approval but anxious not to let the opportunity of good accommodation slip. At this point the obligation is that the accommodation you have provisionally booked is given to no other enquirer without first informing you, while you are in honour bound to release the accommodation as soon as you know you do not need it. Sometimes deadlines are set for provisional bookings, while the reasonable period of uncertainty allowed is likely to depend on the notice involved, but the principle to minimise suspense remains. I would recommend using the provisional period to obtain in writing the exact conditions, facilities available and charges, both the basic charge and any extras, so that when you confirm you know exactly where you are.

Get it in writing

Your contract of hire may take a variety of forms. It can be a simple exchange of letters: make sure this includes all the facilities you are hiring as well as the basic space and the times you need it. Overrunning may involve not only extra expense but also confrontation with another event demanding your accommodation. The same applies, of course, to the form some locations ask you to complete in duplicate and endorse. More and more often, you will be faced with a formal contract. Such contracts often seem full of alarming conditions, not least heavy penalties for cancellation. They should be read carefully, but these conditions are pretty standard and in general must be accepted – they are your protection as well. Most large conference centres ask that a proportion of their hire charge be paid some considerable time before the event and the balance just before or immediately after. University contracts generally ask you to state at some point a guaranteed minimum of delegates and there can be penalties if you have a shortfall. Cancellation is horrendous: if it is due to strikes or even war, you should be covered by insurance (of which more in the next chapter); if it is for lack of support your only remedy is that you are able to pull out in time for the locality to re-let itself. To pursue a harsh policy of compensation for cancellation would be bad for a location's image, so you might escape the full extent of the liability your contract suggests.

I'm sorry to end this chapter on a warning note, but choosing the accommodation for your conference is a serious matter and immediately confronts you with the even more serious subject of my next chapter – the cost.

CHAPTER 4

Finance –
the all-pervasive element

Money, money, money – at no moment, from your first tentative plan to the line drawn under the final account, will it be out of your mind. The theory of conference financing is simple: the fees paid by delegates will cover your costs and, if you're lucky and clever, produce a surplus or profit. But imagine you are simply a group of people with an idea for a conference and the conviction that an audience for it exists: how will you pay for the office space, the typist, the telephone, the postage, publicity, advance on the hire of the hall, a host of incidental expenses, until the fees begin to come in? Without your own institutional cover, some kind of interim finance would have to be found. (Skip the next section if this doesn't apply to you.)

Going it alone
Your first resort might be sponsorship – from industry, governmental or institutional funds, foundations, charitable or other trusts, even a millionaire! You would need to sell your idea to these sponsors as intrinsically important to their particular concerns and of interest to a wide public that they would like to reach. You would need to convince them of the project's financial viability and for this you would have to prepare a very careful and detailed budget. And you would probably have to give them some say in the programme. This support could come in various forms: an immediate cash advance that would enable you to open a bank account; a guarantee against loss; or an undertaking to pay for various items in your budget. In all cases except the first, the agreement to underwrite your project must be such that on the strength of it a bank would allow you to open a loan account.

Going to the bank direct, you would be faced with an even tougher task. Here again, you would have to convince a manager of the viability – particularly the financial viability – of your project, and without a sponsor the loan would have to be personally guaranteed by the borrower or group of borrowers, whose creditworthiness the bank would need to assess. In such a situation, the costing of your conference has an alarming importance, but even under the comforting umbrella of an institution, an office and a bank account, it can give you a few sleepless nights.

Costing: theory and practice

When it comes to costing, once again the theory is simple: add up all possible expenses and divide by the figure below which you feel sure your number will not fall, to give the break-even point, add a little for profit, if you dare, and you have the basis of your conference fee. At Figure 1 I give a draft budget – a fairly detailed and comprehensive one – to remind you, and me, of all the items that may have to be considered. It would be idle to give definite figures here, as by the time you read this chapter they might well be out of date.

These figures, added up, are your basic costs, to which you are committed, whether your numbers are 50 or 500. You decide that you will break even at 250, by which divide the total of your costs. To the resultant figure add the per-head cost of accommodation and catering, not forgetting to include any extra elements for entertaining – a banquet or reception, for instance. Here then, at £xxx, is your conference fee. And at basic costs plus the per-head cost multiplied by the number of delegates, you have the total cost of your conference.

Fixing the fee

At first blush it sounds simple. But immediately there are two questions you need to ask yourself. Is this fee anything like the figure you and your committee believe those you hope to attract would be willing to pay? On what have you based your estimate of the likely minimum number that will attend? Of these two uncertainties, the second is the great unknown and the hazard that you have to face.

Figure 1 The budget

	£	£
Overhead		000
Publicity		000
Printing and postage		000
Hire of halls (projection, public address, etc.)		000
Simultaneous translation (for an international event)		
facilities	000	
translators' fees	000	000
Speakers – say 20		
Fees – to be negotiated	000	
Presence at conference – catering at £00 per head	000	
Accommodation, if needed, at £00 per bed night	000	
Travel – calculate fares per head	000	000
Staff at conference		
Presence at conference – catering at £00 per head	000	
Accommodation, if needed, at £00 per bed night	000	
Travel – from home or office, per head	000	000
Extracurricular activities – visits, transport		000
Insurance		000
Consultancy fee		000
Miscellaneous social – guests, flowers, toastmaster for banquet, disco, cabaret		000
Contingencies and bad debts		000
Direct costs		£00,000
250 delegates at £00 (catering & accommodation costs) per head		£000,000
Total cost of conference		£000,000

Your fee to break even at 250 will be your *total* costs divided by 250. Profit begins when your numbers exceed this.

The level of the fee needs to be in your mind right from the start – which is why I said money will be one of your earliest thoughts – as it is a determining factor both in the level of your conference and its size. If you are concerned with an established event there is a precedent to go by: stick to this as closely as possible and if an increase in fee is necessary keep it, if possible, below the current rate of inflation – unless you are able to demonstrate that you are giving something different, of higher standard and better value than ever before. For a one-off event, compare the price with competitors and test the feel of the market. Go back again and again to your expenses – the only area over which you are potentially in control – to make sure they won't run away with you, and, trusting to the quality and timeliness of the programme and your guess about numbers, back your hunch for the price the market will bear.

The numbers game

For numbers, again precedents tell. A well-established event – a series, an annual conference – will probably show a fairly constant attendance, but even here a fluctuation of as much as a hundred can occur and make havoc with your budget. For a one-off event, with all your skill and experience there is no guarantee that your guess is right.

Later in this chapter I shall talk about insurance, but no policy covers this hazard although I feel I am being less than constructive in saying so. One can say, perhaps, that with the right time and topic, place and price, it should not arise, but that is being a little facile, like being against sin. For a small event, if the bookings persistently fail, it is probably not too damaging or expensive – certainly cheaper than running at a loss – to cancel; for a large conference, so much has already been invested in time, effort, prestige and financial commitments of various kinds that the dilemma is acute indeed. Some of the expedients to minimise the disaster might be to change to less ambitious accommodation; to eliminate all 'frills' (receptions, visits, alternative sessions); to reduce your printing programme (though not your publicity), giving thought to cheaper methods of reproduction; to cut down on overseas speakers (if this option is still open) or the number of your own staff attending the event; to try to recoup your deficit by the sale of the proceedings. This kind of situation is the conference organiser's nightmare and puts all your resourcefulness and fortitude on trial.

Insurance

In these uncertain and dangerous days insurance is a must and though your first feeling may be that it doesn't cover the risk that is perpetually before your eyes – lack of support from your public – just consider all the other hazards that are outside your control. Cancellation or abandonment (and hence an obligation to refund delegates' and exhibitors' fees) can be due to strikes, bomb attacks or scares, failure of power supplies, non-availability of the venue due to fire, student sit-ins, non-appearance of principal speakers, infectious diseases, to name just some of the possibilities. As mentioned in my previous chapter, conference locations impose quite severe financial penalties for cancellation or if for any reason – for instance, a transport strike – you are unable to vacate the premises by the time stipulated in the hiring contract. Loss or damage to property – not only your own but also any property hired or lent to you – is your responsibility (and this could involve some pretty pricey items, such as stage sets, exhibition stands, audiovisual equipment, furnishings). You would also be held liable for any loss or damage to the structure or contents of the location during your tenancy even if it was caused by someone else, like a sub-contractor or delegate. You need, too, to be adequately protected for the legal and contractual liabilities for claims arising from injuries to employees or others and all third-party property damage. A company specialising in exhibition and conference insurance is your best bet. They will not only know the hazards and the protection needed, but also their expertise is likely to ensure a competitive cost. Expo-Sure Limited is the company patronised by ACE (Association of Conference Executives) and their conference and exhibition insurance facility was devised in association with ACE. There are others.

Back to the budget

Although at every point you will be watching your costs and trying to keep them down, in doing your addition it is always wise to level up (like prices!) rather than level down. However careful you are, costs are inclined to grow, and this gives you a little leeway. Quotations will be made with or without a percentage for service (which of course you must include) and then there is the question of Value Added Tax. If your organisation is registered for VAT you know all about this and have worked out how it affects your costing operation: as I have practised it, because I was both paying and reclaiming, it could be ignored in my calculations. If you are not VAT-registered it is, alas, simply an addition to your costs. There is of course a statutory level at which VAT registration becomes compulsory, and as to whether your conference fee is subject to VAT, I have noticed that practice varies and HM Customs and Excise alone can give you an authoritative ruling.

Costs – a close-up
Turning now to the direct costs listed in my specimen budget (Figure 1). If conference organising is your institution's main activity or you are a conference department in an organisation, you know all about overheads. They cover, of course, the basic cost of keeping you going as an operating unit – accommodation, salaries, office services, equipment, telephone, postage, etc. – and must be met by your conference income during the year. There are various formulas for calculating how much overhead to allot to a budget. You may work on the basis of a fixed sum per conference day – this works best when you are organising a regular flow of conferences of rather similar scale – or you may relate it in a rather more *ad hoc* way to the overall budget, making your overhead, for instance, equal to your direct costs. It is very important not to chisel away your overhead in an attempt to keep down the fee: after all, whatever happens, this expense has to be met. At the same time, don't destroy the delicate balance of the acceptable fee by making your overhead too high.

Publicity, printing and postage are closely intertwined, so perhaps we can consider them together. Printing is a large item and printing costs are not only high but expand. If you have an in-house printing facility use it to the utmost. Insist on detailed estimates from printers and make careful comparisons; try to foresee what all your printing requirements will be – not only publicity leaflets, programme and registration form, a conference handbook, but invitations to functions, a menu, preprints perhaps. Reprinting is expensive, so be generous in your estimate of numbers. New technology offers cheaper alternatives to traditional printing methods and I shall talk about this in the next chapter. Postage also can escalate. If it isn't part of your overhead you will have to do some real calculation here (and bear in mind how your material might be included with other mailings). Press advertising, if you are thinking of it, can cost a great deal and you will need to check just how much. If you think of including your publicity shot with some other organisation's mailing (a common practice) bear in mind there is generally a fee for this. Keep something in reserve in this part of the budget in case a special boost to your drive is needed – an extra mail shot, an advertisement, a telephone campaign.

The hire of halls and facilities is a pretty straightforward item – the hire charges should have been clearly stated and you simply add them in. Projection and public address systems need a bit more thought. As the possibilities for demonstration and audiovisual presentation develop they become more complicated, more likely to demand a full-time operator, and more expensive. Simultaneous translation is an enormously costly option. Accommodation that provides this facility will not be cheap; the fees to interpreters are high and if they are not local you may have to pay travel and hotel costs. All these items need to be scrutinised with care and the figure you allot to this part of your budget should not be skimped.

Speakers' expenses can vary so widely, and there is no invariable practice for meeting them, that I can only say be very sure in your own mind what you have let yourself in for and make quite clear to your speakers what you are offering. The question of fees and their level is for each conference organisation to decide and negotiate. If you are dealing with a media personality you will probably communicate through an agent and there will be a fat fee. In your own discipline, there is probably a going rate that you can discover. Consultants normally have a time rate, but they will often reduce this for speaking in a conference, which can be valuable publicity for them. In many institutional conferences, fees are neither offered nor expected, but free attendance at the conference and accommodation for as long as is necessary are, I would say, invariable. It is advisable to make the accommodation arrangements for your speakers rather than leaving it to their own initiative. If meals are part of the conference programme you should not have to think about additional subsistence payments, and many hotels will issue a voucher to give to the speakers, stating what they are getting at your expense – generally bed and breakfast. But if speakers have to find their own meals you must face the possibility of expenses claims and you may decide to indicate a rate – which will, of course, ensure that all speakers claim! Travel expenses are almost always met (and so they should be). It is wise to mention at what rate (second class rail, tourist airfare, etc.). You will arrive at a rough idea of this figure by studying railway timetables and from your travel agent. Speakers will also, of course, be guests at any functions or socialising at the conference and this must be included in the cost per head of their presence.

The cost of your staff at the conference is calculated in the same way as for your speakers. You have more control over them and know just how far they are travelling and how, but you'll have to meet every expense they incur. Extracurricular activities, such as visits to places of interest in the neighbourhood, go together with transport. On the transport side you will have to think how to bring your material and documentation (and some of your staff) to the conference place, and may decide to hire a minivan. If large numbers of your delegates will arrive by train, buses to meet them at the railway station (and to return them there at the end of the conference) may be important. You may also need to hire buses to carry your delegates to functions planned as part of the programme. A series of local visits may be part of the programme, in which case the transport for them and any incidental expenses, such as entrance fees, fees for guides, tips, etc., must be included in your budget.

I've already urged insurance on you: the premium will be an item in the budget, and I've also included a consultancy fee, in case you have to buy in expert advice on any aspect of your programme. You should negotiate a price for this.

Also on my list, a 'miscellaneous' entry – guests and entertaining, items such as a toastmaster for your banquet, a disco or cabaret, flowers. This can be a large item or quite a small one, depending on you or your committee and the tradition of your event. The only real necessity is to be warned in advance – when you're calculating the budget, in fact. You must know how many guests to cater for and whether for a drink, for a banquet, for the whole conference; what size and sort of cabaret or other entertainment (and be sure you know the cost; discos don't have to be expensive); how many flowers? This is the spot where a big-hearted director can spring a party on you at the last minute. You need to be forewarned and forearmed against this. Perhaps some of these should come under my last item – 'contingencies and bad debts': the latter I hope I can help you to avoid before this chapter ends.

It will probably have struck you that there is a certain vagueness, not to say volatility, about some of these expenses – you can't, for instance, calculate exactly what your speakers' expenses will be, it is difficult to quibble over their claims. A printer's estimate is not a contract, only an indication. If you make very extensive corrections in proof or increase your print number, your costs will rise. It's a 'guesstimate' that you have, in fact. But in some of the areas of heaviest commitment – the hire of a conference centre or lecture rooms, of equipment, of simultaneous translation facilities and translators' fees, the per-day delegates' rate, the costs of catering, the hotel room rate, the cost of full board at a university – vagueness is not inevitable. You can insist that these costs are set out unequivocally in writing and you should accept them in writing specifically and not any others by implication. Note in doing so any small print; for instance, there may be a higher delegate day rate if your numbers fall below your estimate. I have enlarged on this in the section about contracts in my previous chapter.

Income – and a few optional extras

We've talked so much about expenditure, let's give a thought to income and how to gather it in. Apart from fees from delegates and possibly sponsorship, this could come from the sale of proceedings, advertisements in the conference documents, and the exhibition. Certainly an exhibition can be a money-spinner and, as it will add greatly to the administrative effort, high profitability is one of the main justifications for having it. But exhibitions are subject to many of the same hazards, such as lack of support, as the conference itself, which in my view needs to be viable without it. Most conferences produce proceedings, but their publication is not necessarily a profitable venture. The sale of the proceedings is helped by the conference, as delegates are generally able (and willing) to order copies at a reduced (but for the publisher still commercial) price, or the conference fee may be calculated to include a copy of the proceedings. I don't, however, believe many conferences are saved from financial disaster by the sale of proceedings. Advertisements in conference documents depend largely on whether the audience is seen by the advertisers as a potential market for the goods and services offered. The British Medical Association conference is an example of the kind of event whose documents could be a profitable vehicle for advertisements by manufacturers and suppliers of drugs and medical services – a large conference, presenting a well-targeted audience, the handbook kept for the duration of the conference and constantly studied. These are the conditions that can make the sale of advertising space a real boost to your profits.

The fee
So back to our main source of income – the delegate fee. I've talked about the considerations that will have gone to fixing its level and it goes without saying that every fee must cover its full share of the conference's direct costs and everything that the delegate costs individually in catering, accommodation, transport, entertainment and so forth. I also suggested, in some of the scenarios sketched in the last chapter, what the advantages, from the point of view of collection, of a basic fee with no possible extras or deductions, an all-inclusive composite fee, or an unvarying package could be.

The registration form accompanying your publicity material should ask applicants either to enclose a cheque for the fee with their booking form, give details of their credit account to be charged (if you accept this method of payment), or request an invoice. If your delegates are mostly being paid for by companies or institutions, the invoice will almost always be requested. Remember in your publicity to state clearly to whom cheques should be payable and whether VAT is included in the fee or should be added at the current rate. You may need to give special instructions about payment. For instance, an international conference with a large number of overseas delegates can incur considerable bank charges paying cheques from foreign banks into the conference account. This can be met by specifically asking that overseas payments be made in sterling by the payer's bank to a numbered account of your bank, stating that all charges should be borne by the payer. (Check with your bank about this, as practice can vary.) I would also recommend that all invoices to overseas applicants carry such simple payment instructions.

It is axiomatic, surely, that attendance at the conference depends on prepayment of the fee. If you are dealing with the general public this should always be the case, but if you are a membership organisation it could be undiplomatic or worse to withhold documents or entry to an old and faithful member of whose ability and intention to pay you have no real doubt. There is also the element of good will, which you may feel is worth the loss of a few fees. A matter for judgement, but this is where the item for 'bad debts' in your budget comes in.

Making them pay
Devices for ensuring prompt payment of invoices can include a reduced fee (which must in fact be the economic rate on which your budget is based) up to a given date – say four weeks – before the conference, when a surcharge is imposed. In invoicing you can state that tickets and/or documents and joining instructions will be sent only on receipt of the fee. Whatever you do, there will always be snags and exceptions, and you should allow in your work schedule for a series of chasers after unpaid invoices – I suggest at monthly intervals. And then there will be the late bookers, who cannot in the time raise a cheque or process your invoice (though I suggest stating firmly that bookings after a certain date must be accompanied by a cheque for the full fee). When dealing with an unknown public you must be very wary of this. Payment on arrival can go some way to meet this dilemma; with a familiar audience your risk in the cause of good will is less.

You can to some extent be protected from frivolous bookings by the imposition of a cancellation charge, which covers you also for the expense of handling an abortive application and return of a proportion of the fee. I suggest 20 to 25 per cent of the full fee for this charge. When a cancellation occurs shortly before the event – say two or three weeks, when your tally of numbers has probably been given to the location – there should be no refund. Bear in mind, however, that if the original invoice has not been settled you are unlikely to get any cancellation fee. A further incentive to insist on prompt payment and another area where your bad debts contingency comes in.

I think I must have brought home to you the appropriateness of the title of this chapter, how money pervades every aspect of your conference, how watchful, alert and flexible you need to be, and that you can do with a little luck. Perhaps you should take to yourself Hereward the Wake's motto, 'Watch and pray'.

CHAPTER 5

The publicity campaign

'Blow your own trumpet, make yourself a front page story
No one else will do it for you, so blooooow.'

Though riding naked through the streets like Lady Godiva might seem a trifle excessive (unless your theme is body-building or nudism) it is difficult to oversell a conference. To be effective and also watch your budget, your aim must be to pinpoint your potential audience and beam all your publicity on them. Identifying your audience should, of course, have taken place when first your conference was conceived and the decision to hold it made. Your problem now is to convert this body of anonymous men and women into lists of names and addresses, resorting most probably to the organisations they work for, the societies and institutions to which they belong, the journals that they read.

Name the day

Your first act, as soon as theme, date and place are agreed, should be a simple announcement to alert your members, in any calendar of forthcoming events in your own journal (if you have one), and in others in related fields, and in any publication devoted specifically to forthcoming conferences, such as Aslib's *Forthcoming International Scientific and Technical Conferences*. The timescale for your campaign will vary greatly, depending on whether it is a large event taking months of preparation or a relatively simple and immediate affair. In any case, you should make this first announcement at the earliest possible moment, to stake your claim to the date and start people thinking. From then on you must bring it constantly to their minds.

Calling – for papers or just attention
If a call for papers is part of your programme planning (see page
14) you should allow an extra three months for the operation,
and your next publicity effort would be your call. By this time,
your planning should be pretty well advanced, your main
topics specified and you should be able to give some indication
of the conference fee. The same applies to the preliminary
announcement or 'flyer' that you may like to make at this stage
if you are not thinking of a call for papers. For both these you
will want as wide a circulation as possible and you will have
been researching the membership lists of any bodies with interests related to your theme. You will, of course, mail to your own
members with one of your regular mailings (saving labour and
postage) and hope that you can persuade presumably friendly
institutions to include an insert with their mailing to members,
for which you will generally be asked to pay a fee.

'Direct mail' – rent-a-list
The main thrust of your publicity effort will be this 'direct
mail', as it is technically called, to individuals you hope are
interested. Your task is to find these lists of names. I've mentioned already your own list of members (assuming you are a
membership organisation) and the lists of other organisations in
related fields that you may be able to make use of. From reference books you can compile your own lists – journals from
Benn's Media Directory, academics and university departments
from the *Commonwealth Universities Year Book*; government
departments, research associations and many many others from
Whitaker's Almanack – your own specialist knowledge will
suggest many more. If your conference is an annual event you
probably already have a basic mailing list which you are concerned mainly to up-date or enlarge; if it looks likely to be the
beginning of a series, you will be thinking of building up such a
list for future use. Ideally, you will store this list on a computer,
which makes up-dating easy and enables you to print out the
addresses for your mail shots. Failing this, an alphabetical card
index (not a list) is the most practical for up-dating. In addition,
there are perhaps as many as 3,000 available lists covering
virtually the whole range of professions, industries and many
individual interests compiled by companies and institutions,

which can be rented for a fee. *The Direct Mail Data Book* (Gower Press) lists many of these. The procedure is that you give your material to the list owners, who collate, envelope and despatch it, charging you for postage and handling.

More help with the mail

A mailing of thousands from your own office is in itself a major task. You may, of course, be on to all the dodges – already have a franking machine and a free collection of mail by your local post office every day. But if you do not enjoy such facilities it is worth looking at how the Post Office could help you. For instance, rebates on an increasing scale are offered for large postings of second-class mail – and with the cost of postage this is not to be sneezed at. *A Guide to Effective Direct Mail*, published by the Post Office, tells you about this and other offers and is worth a look even if much of it will not apply to your case. Without much office or staff back-up, it might also be worth considering using a postal service, such as many mailing houses provide, to collate your material into envelopes and post it. Names of such services can be obtained from the Direct Mail Producers' Association, 34 Grand Avenue, London N10 3BP. Tel. 01 883 7229. Finally, for help with envelope stuffing, Old People's and Handicapped Persons' Workshops are cheap and reliable and can often be tracked down through the Welfare Department of your local Town Hall.

The distribution of the call for papers or of the flyer might be accompanied by a preliminary press release, sent to the journals whose readers you hope to reach – a copy of the notice and a brief paragraph for inclusion in the journal's editorial columns (you hope).

The response to the call for papers or flyer will give you a rough – very rough – idea of the kind of interest you can expect. Submissions in response to a call for papers generally come in just before or after the closing date. It is hard to say how the response to this call reflects the general interest in your conference and the likelihood of people to attend. Even a flyer which specifically asks for an expression of interest is not a very reliable guide – people simply will not commit themselves months ahead and consequently prefer to keep silent. But your call or announcement alerts them to your conference and it may well get 'pencilled in' to their forward planning.

Main programme – main impact

Your publicity should make its maximum impact with the issue of the main programme announcement, accompanied by a registration form. This can be timed from six months before the event but can be less, of course, with a shorter run-up period. The very real advantage of long notice could be lost, however, if you are not able to follow up this wide distribution with later mailings, if needed, and with developing write-ups about the event. This is the moment, too, when press coverage can be most effective. The programme can be accompanied by a more informative press release and an address whence more information can be obtained. At any time, too, after publication of this programme you may take up advertising space in the carefully selected press at which you are directing your efforts. Press advertising is comparatively expensive (you must decide when drawing up your budget what can be afforded) but it is an effective means of publicising your project and, if you can afford two series of advertisements, one on publication of the programme and one three or four weeks before the event, I believe it would be money well spent.

Once the programme with registration form is out, bookings should start to come in and you will get a feel of what the response will be. Unfortunately, as the tendency to book late increases, this won't be very conclusive for some time, and you will need to be on the alert to plug any gaps in your campaign. You may take time to write personal letters with the programme, you can ask interested friends to display programmes in their departments or offices, to talk about the project, to bring it to the attention of staff, pupils, colleagues, contacts, employees. You may see scope for a small poster, or even a large one, for display on noticeboards in offices, common rooms, places of work.

The publicity material – your message

The importance of your publicity material – what you say, how you say it – can't be overstressed; it describes what you are offering and, like handwriting, reveals something about the quality of the conference and about you.

Content first
For the preliminary announcement all you need is subject, date, place, originating body and contact for further information. When it comes to the flyer or call for papers you need, in addition, a title, a descriptive paragraph about the conference, whether or not it's residential, and some indication of the fee.

I've seen hours spent trying to arrive at an arresting title, and it is important – at least, a bad title can be positively off-putting. But your aim should be to express concisely – and if you're lucky euphoniously and wittily – just what your conference is about. 'Microprocessors and Intelligence', 'Getting the Most out of EURONET', 'Term Banks for Tomorrow's World' are good (without being in the least snappy) because they do just that. 'HAZMAT – Hazardous Materials' really does have brevity and punch, but the trouble with so many arresting acronyms is their ambiguity and the long explanatory subtitle required.

The all-important descriptive paragraph needs to say, preferably in one sentence, what the conference is about and to go on to state equally concisely the expertise on which it draws; its aims and how it proposes to achieve them; to whom it is addressed; and the benefits that participants should derive from attending. Here again, the crisper and more direct the approach to the reader the better.

A call for papers should go into as much detail as possible about the programme, stating the main session heads and the subjects to be covered, and mentioning any keynote speakers already secured and their topics. If there is to be an exhibition or a book of proceedings this might also be stated. Finally, for the flyer you will need a form to be returned by those interested, asking for the programme and registration form in due course, and possibly giving an idea of how likely the respondent is to make a booking.

For the main programme, I would suggest the following. Your title page should carry the name of your organisation, the conference logo (if you have one), title, date and place, and the descriptive paragraph – which can be the same as the one devised for the call for papers or flyer. At this point, too, you should mention your sponsors, if there are others beside yourself, and you may like to list your organising committee – this can help your cause if it includes some distinguished names. I would introduce the main text of the announcement by listing the chairs and speakers alphabetically, showing their affiliations, and then set out the programme, naming the sessions in the order, on the days and at the times (morning or afternoon) that they will take place, with subjects or, if you have them, titles of the papers and their speakers. The section of the programme with practical information can have a paragraph about location and accommodation – for the sessions, catering and residence. If you need to give information about travel or hotel accommodation – e.g. the hotel booking service or travel agent appointed for the conference – this is the place to mention it. In this programme you will want to announce the exhibition – if you are having one – and, of course, any social events or related visits, all of which are selling points. Finally, of course, the paragraph about fees and what they include, and the registration form. (A checklist of main programme contents is given in Appendix 3.)

You will design your registration form to give you the information you need about the delegate and his or her requirements in the form best adapted to your record system – for instance a file, under surname or name of organisation or a computer program. A simple illustration of such a form (Appendix 4) conveys my meaning: the delegate should be asked to state on the form whatever you need to know, from membership status to travel intentions. You can think of your own variations on this theme. I know this sounds rather a lot. Paradoxically it is important to keep the leaflet moderate in size, crisp and succinct, while the more you can say about the programme, arrangements and price the easier it is for delegates to decide to come and the fewer questions need answering.

This is the material, with variations, that you will use in your advertisements, press releases and subsequent write-ups. The phrases in the descriptive paragraph will find their way into your press release, expanded with the names of speakers and titles of sessions. The descriptive paragraph could perhaps be used as it stands in your advertisements, where brevity will be important. Another adaptation could provide the text for a poster if you decide to produce one. Variety in subsequent write-ups can be achieved by highlighting one particular aspect of the programme, but having found the exact expression of your meaning you won't find it easy to say it in any very markedly different way. That however is not important: driving home the message is what counts.

Style
In the physical presentation of your material lies your greatest opportunity for innovation. The range of printed matter nowadays is so wide and sophisticated it is probably lucky that expense is quite a constraint. If your organisation has its own printing facility you will obviously use it and adapt to what it can do. Without this, you have a number of options.

Copy can be produced in-house using a typewriter or a word processor or computer with wp software that is linked to a letter-quality printer (i.e. one fitted with a daisywheel or golf-ball). Many of these machines have more than one typeface and headings and titles can be dropped in using Letraset or another dry transfer system. A glance in the *Yellow Pages* under 'Printers' reveals how easy it will be to have this copy reproduced. Here you will follow up any personal recommendations you may have. Failing this, you should discuss your needs with one or two picked from the list and see which comes up with the best answer and price. The same people will probably be able to help you if you want your programme typeset. Many of them have quite a range of typefaces and some have a design facility also. In this case, of course, you would discuss your needs with them, see specimen layouts, artwork, paper and coloured inks and papers. Nor are illustrations ruled out. These should be produced by you 'same size' – i.e. the size they are to be reproduced. Line drawings are the most satisfactory (and the cheapest) for this purpose, but photographs need not be ruled out.

Using a word processor or computer wp package to originate text can provide many advantages. It is especially useful for producing documents that require constant revision and updating before they are finished, but also allows you to tailor a store of information (e.g. a list of names and addresses) to a number of different purposes with great ease. One major advantage of putting your conference handbook on disk is that the disk can be sent to a printer and converted for phototypesetting, thus cutting out the time and expense of re-keying by a typesetter. You will need to find a printer whose equipment can 'read' your disk then agree on whether the typesetting codes will be added by the printer or entered during the initial keying. The latter option is cheaper and should not prove difficult for a competent wp operator.

A few rather basic considerations as you start to design your printed material. Size is important – think of the envelopes you will be using (perhaps you have a hoard of a particular size you could use up!). Envelopes nowadays are ruinously expensive and it is worth adapting to them. Weight is also a consideration, postage costing what it does. There is an argument for keeping all your printed matter the same size (envelopes again). Collating pages of printed matter is labour-intensive – consider the possibility of printing on a large sheet and folding. But if you do this make sure that the printing machine can carry the size of sheet. If you have a tear-off registration slip it is important that its back should carry no text. A second colour adds to the expense. Save money by providing faultless copy. Exercise restraint in the use of typefaces – too much variety looks a mess. Never forget legibility – size of type comes in here and the colour of the printing: light ink on light paper is hard to read.

Suitability to your organisation and aptness for your theme are the best criteria for the design of your printed material. If you use an outside designer make very sure he or she is well briefed and is aware of these criteria. I would advocate a house style for all the printed material for your conference. If you have a logo or special motif, use it on all the printed matter, with the same artwork, typeface and colour for the flyer or call for papers, for the main programme, and for the handbook if you have one. Maintaining the image, keep the logo or motif on your advertisements and handbills and possibly on invitations and menus as well. If your conference is one of a series, you can emphasise this by introducing variations into a basic design. For instance, the logo and style could remain constant but with an individual visual reference to the theme and perhaps a different colour for the whole set of papers. It is always worth keeping a file of your artwork, for possible use in the future or even for a reprint, though you will aim not to need this.

As you see, there is great scope for variety and invention here and to make the most of your ideas I would recommend equipping yourself with a good basic guide. *The Presentation of Information* (Aslib) contains much useful advice on the design and production of printed matter and is written especially for those for whom these tasks form part of some other job. I will simply end this section on the very practical note of your print number. Looking at my suggestions for mailing earlier in this chapter you can see it may be pretty formidable. Never underestimate: it is the design and setting that cost money, not the size of the run.

Flight of the imagination

A publicity campaign is above all an imaginative exercise and no holds – from TV to T-shirts – are barred. TV advertising is expensive but as channels increase you should explore it, and if you can get mentioned on a TV programme you can feel very pleased with yourself. Local radio can often be interested at the time of the event, interviewing your more notable speakers or reporting on sessions of topical or controversial interest. To be always on the alert for opportunities to talk, to hand out programmes, to push your project, is the best advice I can give.

CHAPTER 6

Putting on the show

Of all the elements that combine to make a successful conference, the programme and its presentation are the top. It is your
biggest challenge, an area which you cannot control completely and which attracts the harshest criticism – some of it
unjustified and simply prejudiced, for tastes in conference
programmes vary, as in everything else. It is fashionable to
suggest that the so-called traditional conference of papers,
presentations and discussion is dying, to be replaced by 'a
series of three-dimensional "landscapes" in which delegates
discover new truths . . . finely tuned, razor-sharp excursions
into the minds of delegates', while computer conferencing
may even put an end to attending conferences at all.

If I believed that I wouldn't have bothered to write this
book; but the dictionary does define a conference as 'meeting
for discussion, exchange of views' and this exchange is not
always easy to stage-manage. I hope I can make some suggestions in this chapter as to how it can be achieved.

The *mise en scène*
The physical setting of your sessions is the area in presenting
your programme where you have the most control. You will
have given it a lot of thought when you chose your location
and I have talked at some length about your minimum needs
and the various types of room you may find yourself using,
from custom-built lecture theatre to converted ballroom, to
large or small seminar rooms, through formality to extreme
informality. I have also discussed various arrangements of
these rooms, to create the most satisfactory conditions to
achieve your programme's aim. As you planned your programme you will have thought how to put it across: in a
plenary session, with parallel sessions – how many and on

what scale? With discussion sessions or workshops – how many and of what size? And your location will have been chosen to meet your needs. Your task now is to make the best of the accommodation you have.

To be able to see, to be comfortably seated, not cold but also not too hot (stuffiness induces sleep however fascinating the speaker) should not be in question. If you are showing slides or films, the screen must be large enough for every delegate to see it properly and high enough not to be blocked by the rows in front (see Appendix 5). For a smaller meeting, various different arrangements may be particularly conducive to attention and communication: classroom-style, seated at small tables (with writing materials); for a group of up to thirty or so at a meeting involving discussion and decision-taking, seating at a round, square or oblong table; U-shaped, which has proved itself in teaching situations; finally, theatre-style for large numbers of delegates. In this situation there should be a platform for the speakers and ideally the seats should be fixed to a tiered or sloping floor (see Appendix 6). If you are using a converted ballroom or any hall without a rake for your plenary session, the elevation of the platform, so that it is visible from the back of the room, will be specially important. The shape of your hall is also a consideration. Long and narrow from back to front is less than ideal; true theatre-shaped, wider than deep, or shell-shaped, is ideal. The screen or screens will be along the back wall, or possibly angled at the sides (see Appendix 7).

Preference and circumstances will dictate the arrangement of the platform. You may like to have all the speakers on the platform for the whole duration of the session. Unless you expect them all to be involved in any questions and discussion I think it is preferable only to have one speaker up at a time – and kinder and more relaxing for the other speakers. The person chairing the session will be seated at a table, generally centre-stage, provided with microphones, from which he or she will introduce the session and the speaker. The latter will either talk from this same table or from a lectern, also provided with a microphone (unless you are into neck microphones). The obligatory carafe of water and glasses should be on the table and a further glass of water on the lectern. If you are showing slides and the hall will be in darkness, be sure that there is a light on the lectern so that the speaker can read his or her script (if you're not giving autocue!). There also should be a pointer – sometimes a long stick, sometimes a device called a laser that points with a spot of light. The lectern may be provided with various controls for the projection, or instructions to change the slides may be given verbally. Lighting is usually controlled by the projectionist – dimming when slides are shown, returning to full strength when the visuals or the presentation end. If there is no projectionist, you will have to be responsible for this. Name cards for the chair and speakers are elementary. They should stand on the table, each in front of the speaker concerned for quick identification, and you must make sure that the name of the speaker is on the lectern as he or she speaks. When you have a panel session and all speakers are on the platform, this labelling is particularly helpful to the audience.

In smaller sessions – workshops, discussion groups, etc. – the setting will be more informal, but it needs to be carefully arranged. There should still be labels for the chair, speakers and panel members – you may even want to identify all the participants, but they should in any case be wearing their badges (of which more later). The person chairing the session will still be most comfortable seated at a table; the speaker may be happier talking from a lectern (perhaps a table lectern) or may prefer to move about freely (a microphone should not be needed). Speakers will probably prefer to operate their own slides, if they have any to show, and this is the kind of occasion when an overhead projector comes in. You will have carefully checked the position of the screen and also of the projectors themselves. Felt-tipped pens for writing on the overhead transparencies and on the flipchart (if provided) and chalk for the blackboard should all be available. Don't forget the carafe of water and glasses, scatter round ashtrays (unless you've been able to impose a smoking ban) and remember that pencils and paper will be needed by the participants.

Technology – the great added dimension
New-style conference presentation relies very heavily on technology – projectors, film, television, videos and the linking of these into audiovisual programmes. But quite simple presentations need careful attention to what might be called the

'hardware' of your production and before looking at the far trickier problem of dealing with your human material, I will talk a little about this.

First of all, don't forget the microphone. In all larger halls this is necessary and it comes in various forms: the standing microphone, either on the floor or on the desk; the microphone fixed to the lectern; the one you hold in your hand (like a pop star crooning); and, best of all, the neck microphone, which enables you to move around freely and avoids the problem of speaking away from the mike. This is a simple form of voice amplification, but many halls have a public address system wired in and amplifiers sited strategically down the room. An added advantage of such a wired-in PA system is that you can plug a tape-recorder directly into it and get a much more satisfactory recording than if you have to rely on your recorder to pick up the naked sound.

A marvellous device, if you want to pamper your speaker and, incidentally, greatly enhance his or her presentation, is the autocue, a closed-circuit television system which enables him or her to do away with notes or script and look directly at the audience. How? The typewritten speech is fed at the desired speed by an operator through a script-scanning unit behind the scenes, and relayed to one or more visual displays sited conveniently for the speaker. The text is reflected upwards from TV monitors onto one-way glass screens which the speaker can read easily but which are invisible to the audience.

While we are about the sound side of things, I will also mention simultaneous translation systems, although fortunately they are hardly part of normal presentation. These are electronic systems of great complexity and high cost. It is possible to install one in a hall not so provided, at a price (I've done it), but I strongly advise against. You are not likely to have the expertise that would enable you to assess the various possibilities on offer and there is endless scope for operational faults and breakdowns. If your programme needs simultaneous translation you must insist on a hall where the system is permanently installed and its functioning familiar to the technicians on the spot.

The simplest forms of visual aid are the blackboard and the flipchart, both effective for really small, informal meetings and discussion groups. To some extent the same applies to the overhead projector, a very popular aid that again has the advantage of informality. The speaker can stand by the machine and move his or her own transparencies, or add to and amend them, or even write them afresh as he or she talks. Most locations provide overhead projectors and many speakers prefer them (perhaps because the transparencies are not too difficult or costly to produce), but they are not really very suitable for large lecture halls, the main problem being that it is difficult to get enough distance between the projector and the screen to throw up a large enough image. Transparencies for overhead projection can be prepared manually, using felt-tipped pens in various colours, or photographically. Printed text and diagrams can be transferred to clear or tinted film by almost every make of plain paper office copier. Lettering should be set in capitals and lower case in an easy-to-read typeface and *it must not be too small.* On most projectors the usable transparency is 250mm × 250mm, which means that the individual height of a letter should be not less than between 5mm and 10mm, if the image is to be readable over the whole auditorium. Incidentally, audiovisual experts maintain that if people are to see details clearly, the maximum distance between audience and image should be no greater than eight times the height of the projected image. (See Appendix 5.) This should be borne in mind when the picture image of transparencies, slide or film is measured and that ratio should be adhered to if possible.

The most used, best loved and still the most effective visual aid is the 35mm slide, and its already great potential can be enhanced by using two or even more projectors at the same time, thus enormously increasing the variety and scope of the presentation. The content and quality of the slide is, of course, of the greatest importance, and though one imagines first the beautiful coloured slides of art and travel, graphs and drawings and lettering can be satisfactorily reproduced provided a few simple rules are observed. (You will find these in the specimen note to speakers at Appendix 8.) Slides need to be professionally produced and they are shot with sophisticated cameras which are invariably expensive. Now a new technology, computer graphics, can create images of bar charts, graphs, text and logos in full colour, quickly and sometimes more cheaply, without the use of a draughtsman or drawing board. This is a process which uses a computer to reproduce graphic images – letters, symbols, etc. – on a screen. Using a computer programme, the operator can experiment with sizes, styles and proportion, manipulate shapes and colours, and when the desired combination has been found, the image can be preserved on a slide. With skill and imagination, repeated shots and fade changes, brilliant effects can be achieved for slide shows and from these slides video recordings or film can be made. With such techniques available, you might do well to allow an item in your budget to help your speakers, both technically and financially, to illustrate their papers really well.

In its simplest form – one machine only – slide projection is easy to operate provided the slides are numbered and given to the projectionist or placed in the carousel in the right order, the right way up and facing the right way! Instructions to change slides can either be given to the projectionist verbally – 'Next slide, please' – or a remote control device may be provided, enabling the speakers to operate the changes themselves. There are also automatic tape/slide systems that can be operated at the press of a single button.

Remote control is still possible in a two-projector presentation – though it takes a lot of concentration by the speaker – but when you come to multi-projector presentations, expert help and an operator are advisable if not essential. I suggest this also applies when you start to explore some of the developing possibilities in audiovisual presentation. The 16mm film has, of course, been with us for a long time. Making a film is an expert business and not cheap, but libraries of films on almost every subject exist and these can be hired and woven into a presentation along with other visuals, or used to set the scene, illustrate an argument or drive home a conclusion. More exciting, and with a potential that could revolutionise visual presentation in conferences, is the video. Now that video recording of television programmes and live events has improved so greatly, while the new generation of TV projectors makes screen sizes up to twenty-four feet wide possible, projected video can be used for audiences of 500 or more and can show combinations of live and pre-recorded material such as one sees daily on TV screens. Hitherto, all audiovisual material used at conferences and meetings, whether slide, film or video, had to be pre-recorded, but the combination of video and TV that I have just described gave birth to the realisation that live video, a rendering of what is happening now, on the stage, can have even more impact. For instance, a live picture of your speaker could be projected onto the screen so that the audience can see his or her expression and, in a large hall, feel a more personal rapport; demonstrations on the platform can be shown on the screen as they happen (this is an invaluable development for a technological topic) and supporting slides or pre-recorded film could be shown on the same screen; images of delegates as they ask questions could be projected onto the screen, as could the image of an absent speaker (this, of course, is the thin edge of the teleconferencing wedge).

Once TV, video and computer get going there is very little limit to the possibilities and what I have told you is no more than a sketch of avenues you might explore. In such exploration, a sense of proportion is a valuable asset, as there is a danger in all this proliferation of becoming gimmicky. I cannot resist a word of warning, born of sometimes bitter experience, even though I realise it reveals a certain ambivalence in my attitude to the wonders of technology. However theoretically simple your audiovisual requirements, there is the perpetual hazard that the technology won't work. Slides, although apparently of the right dimension, don't fit the carousel; the film snaps in the projector; the bulb of the overhead projector blows. For this reason my strongest advice is, don't go it alone, enlist as much expert help as you can, both in creating any sort of visual programme and in presenting it. And in the matter of equipment, whether buying or hiring, the same applies. This is not the place to name specific equipment by particular makers – in any case the field is developing so rapidly that my recommendations would soon be out of date – but, as a general principle, do not be fobbed off with the second best for economy's sake. For brightness, sharp definition and minimum distortion in your picture image, you need good projection lenses. The quality and whiteness of your screen also have an important effect on the picture image. Fortunately, there are sources of information and advice. The National Audio-Visual Aids Centre provides comprehensive information and instruction, and many Colleges of Further Education offer courses in all aspects of audiovisual presentation. I would recommend any conference organiser to take at any rate a basic course, so that he or she knows at least what the options are and what they involve. For a big presentation, I would always recommend professional help, but if you are engaged with a lot of small teaching conferences and seminars I would advise getting right into the technology and setting up your own audiovisual programmes. Many of these new developments are particularly effective in this more intimate, educational context.

The dramatis personae

Having set your stage and organised the 'props', on with the players – the all-important speakers and chairs, and delegates, if you're aiming at audience participation. What are the commonest complaints about conference sessions? Bad timing, overrunning, starting late; hurried delivery, over-dependence on the script, incomprehensible slides or slides badly shown; presentations inadequately introduced and, still worse, incomplete and without conclusion; speakers sitting during the presentation (but for this there can be good reasons of age or infirmity which do not detract from the quality of the paper); speakers wandering about, turning their backs on the audience, gazing at the ceiling or indeed anywhere except the audience; badly managed discussion, questions inaudible or allowed to wander off the point; sessions inadequately introduced and concluded. Almost all these criticisms are directed at the speakers or chairs, which brings home how much depends on this mixed bunch of only partially controllable men and women.

On the choice of speakers

I talked in my chapter 'The irresistible conference' about finding your speakers, and cannot add much to this. When you have taken all the advice at your disposal, used all your experience and kept your ear to the ground for personal recommendation and reputation until it has almost taken root, you have the problem of assessing how a particular speaker will fit into the ambience of your conference and, finally, you have to take some chances or be stuck forever in your past, in established figures, in *déjà vu*. All the more reason to take trouble about what you can do – the very careful briefing of your speakers and chairs.

A thoroughly detailed guide

An invitation to a speaker should state not only his or her own topic, when and where, but the other speakers and his or her place in the particular session. You should also state the main lines of the programme and its objective, the level of audience and any aspect of the topic that you particularly want emphasised. It is helpful if you can arrange for speakers to see synopses of each others' papers before their contributions are completed. Encourage them to think about the forms their presentations should take, how they might be illustrated, the content of their slides. It would be an advantage if they can manage not to read their papers word for word.

Emphasise that it is very important not to exceed the time allotted. Explain in as much detail as possible how the sessions will be run – that the speakers will be introduced by the chair, that at the end of each paper some minutes are allowed for questions, and how these should be handled (the chair also comes in here). Describe the conditions in which they will be speaking (large plenary session in a raked auditorium with an audience in hundreds; smaller, more informal presentation in a seminar room; round-table discussion or panel). Describe exactly what visual aids are available and ask them to tell you what they will need. Warn them if you are using simultaneous translation and point out that this demands a considerably slower delivery to enable the interpreters to keep pace. At this point, too, you should remind them of the situation regarding the proceedings – if they will be published, when you need the text of the papers, and in what form. The publication of conference proceedings is discussed in chapter 11 (pp. 104 – 105); don't forget that such a publication is often the outcome of, and has a bearing on, instructions to speakers and chairs.

'Time, gentlemen, please' – the chair's role

The chair is a vital ingredient in the session's success. His or her first task is to introduce the theme in a few well chosen words (and I mean a few – say how long there is for this) and follow up by introducing the speaker(s), outlining in a sentence or two the salient points about the speaker's background and qualifications in the subject of his or her paper.

The chair is responsible for ensuring that speakers do not overrun their allotted time. Sometimes warning lights are provided in the auditorium, otherwise the chair must be prepared to interrupt. The discussion period can look threatening, with the fear of never a word from the floor. This doesn't often occur, but the chair will be wise to have one or two questions prepared, just to 'set the tambourine a-rolling'. He or she should instruct the audience how the discussion will be handled; if there are roving microphones, tell people to use them, to state their questions briefly and to say who they are. For clarity's sake, it is often as well to repeat the question, possibly rephrasing it. The chair will have to prevent the question getting bogged down in irrelevancies and know when to move on to the next one. Finally, at the end of the session, a few words of summing up and thanks to the speakers.

Briefing the speakers and chairs
These detailed and in places rather obvious-seeming instructions are best conveyed to your speakers and chairs in a formal note, an example of which appears at Appendix 8. This is drawn mainly from my experience at Aslib and of course you will adapt it to your individual needs. I have drafted it as a communication addressed directly to the individual speaker, with the title of his or her paper, its time and duration to be filled in by you, as I think this is more likely to be read than a more general 'Note for Speakers'. I have also attached to it a form for return to you asking for the summary of the paper, projection requirements, biographical and other details that you may need. It may seem superfluous, even a little presumptuous, to send such instructions to experienced speakers, but the more information you give the easier it is to produce exactly the right paper, and the tone of your covering letter can make your note sound helpful rather than peremptory.

Preparation is perhaps the keyword, and use of the new technology described earlier in this chapter underlines this very heavily. However apparently simple your presentation, if you are able to rehearse your speakers in the hall with your projection and projectionist, jump at the chance. A meeting of speakers and chairs before the proceedings begin. to run through all the points of organisation, is invaluable (in fact, I'd like to say essential). A full-scale rehearsal in the hall would be better still, and you really must insist on chairs and speakers gathering in the hall fifteen minutes before the start of a session, to make sure they know their way about the platform and how the session will be run, where the visual aids are (and, of course, to hand over their slides to the projectionist, with any instructions), and to make sure the microphones work. The skimping of these preparations is the cause of many a less-than-perfect show.

Making discussion work
The third element that I mentioned in our cast list was the audience. As this leads on to my final thought in this chapter – the greater involvement of the whole delegate body in the conference theme – I will talk for a little about discussion sessions and then throw out a few ideas about the interaction problem.

'Too little discussion' is a common complaint and yet the points raised are often so trivial and irrelevant that one feels they would have been better left unsaid. The fact is that discussion is not too appropriate in a large audience and has to be skilfully stage-managed. One device is the 'planted' question and, as I've said already, the wise chair will have a few in reserve. Sometimes it is possible to ask delegates to submit written questions in advance, and boxes for written questions, prominently displayed during the conference, can produce quite an interesting return. In a large hall, roving microphones must be pressed on the questioners – nothing is more tedious than questions you can't hear – and if the chair briefly repeats the question, so much the better. However hard you try, the large audience and inevitable formality discourage many and detract from the essential spontaneity of true discussion, while it is sometimes difficult to prevent the over-extrovert, the aggressive or the bore from holding the floor.

In a small session, many of these problems disappear. Nevertheless, specific discussion sessions need to be carefully prepared. I believe the discussion leader should open with a few remarks deliberately designed to be controversial, and a

number of points for discussion should be given to the participants, if possible in advance. A good discussion leader or
chair will try to elicit the views of all – or as many as possible –
of those in his or her group and encourage them to co-operate in
producing some kind of agreed statement at the end of the
session.

A possible formula for interaction
I think that complaints about insufficient or ineffective discussion are due to a slightly more general malaise: delegates desire
greater interaction and involvement in the whole conference
process without, however, being able or sometimes even willing to do much about it themselves. It is, however, essential to
their happiness – and continuing desire to come to your conferences – that they should find the people they want to talk to,
the answers to the questions they brought with them or which
the conference topic inspired, that the dialogues started should
be continued, and any misunderstandings dispelled. The lists
of participants you will have issued are one means of making
this meeting of minds possible, but in *Transnational Associations* (1/1980) A.J.N. Judge has written at length about a process
he describes as 'Participant Interaction Messaging', which he
believes attacks the problem more directly. He writes at length
and describes many permutations of the process, but I'm sure he
would not mind my passing on some of his suggestions for you
to think about.

He recommends a message board for the exchange of messages between participants; not a new idea, and many's the
board that has gone unnoticed. But publicise this facility, by a
verbal announcement at the beginning of the conference, or
better still in an explanatory sheet with the conference documents, accompanied perhaps by some blank cards to encourage
participation. Invite your delegates to use this message system
to suggest additional subjects they would like discussed; to
comment on points made by speakers or in discussion; to
address questions to specific speakers; to remark on the conference documents or the programme as a whole (there could be
some uncomfortable but perhaps useful home truths here!); to
raise initiatives on which they are seeking support. There could
also be invitations to meet informally to discuss particular

points; organisational queries or complaints; comments on previous messages. Message boxes should be prominently displayed at key points and it would be the task of the conference
organiser to empty them from time to time and – the crucial
element in the operation – to disseminate the messages. Mr
Judge suggests this could be done in the form of a reproduced
bulletin distributed to all the delegates once or twice a day –
depending on the number of messages, of course! Displaying
the cards on the message board would be an alternative, but I
doubt if it would attract as much attention. The hope is that
messages would provoke further messages, meetings and inter-
acting groups, and my suggestion is that points raised or questions submitted should, when appropriate, be taken in the
sessions themselves. This would add to the demands on
speakers and chairs as well as on the conference organisation,
while issuing and distributing a bulletin would be quite labour-
intensive; but supposing it caught on and created a dynamic
and highly interactive conference? Perhaps it sparks off in you
some even more brilliant innovation for the presentation of your
programme. I leave it to you!

CHAPTER 7

The lighter side

'All work and no play makes Jack a dull boy'

A conference without a social programme is like gingerbread without the gilt. This lighter side is very important – to create an atmosphere of welcome and warmth, breaking down shyness and reserve among the delegates; to provide an antidote to the seriousness of the sessions and literally, perhaps, a breath of fresh air; and to meet the ever rising expectations of your public.

No wonder expectations are high – so much is on offer. Here are some of the possibilities that researching this chapter has brought to my notice: an 'Edwardian Evening with Old-Time Music Hall Entertainment'; lunch or dinner on a riverboat (with dancing, too, perhaps, or gambling); champagne in a safari park watching the animals play; a medieval banquet in an old tithe barn with court jester, fire-eater and juggler, and a baron of beef served to a fanfare of trumpets; not to mention, of course, dinner with a duke in his stately home. . . With imagination and a large budget almost anything is possible, but personally I would call on an expert in such conference entertainments to negotiate and arrange such a Rolls-Royce event. At a more down-to-earth level I have seen and had a hand in arranging a musical evening at Haddo House; a flowing of wonderful wine in a German art gallery; a reception with bagpipes and reels (not danced by delegates) in Stirling Castle; dinner and dancing in Sheffield Art Gallery; drinks in the Sheldonian Theatre; more drinks in Castle Howard; dinner in the Assembly Rooms at Bath and under the Raphaels in the Victoria and Albert Museum; and more civic receptions than I can name.

From this last list you will see that there are plenty of possibilities; you may also have noticed that this is an area where sponsorship comes in. Many cities have a policy of offering civic hospitality to incoming conferences. For this you have to apply, usually to the Lord Mayor's Secretary – a process that you may feel is a little pushy but is simply a formality that has to be observed. The application is considered and almost always approved by the City Council, the form this hospitality should take having been discussed with you beforehand. In the past, I have experienced incredible generosity; in today's harder times such a reception generally takes the form of drinks either before or after dinner, with the party received by the Lord Mayor or his Deputy. The standard of hospitality within this format varies widely and so does the interest, which can depend a good deal on the setting: for instance, Norwich Castle (a huge Norman keep), with Cotmans and Cromes on the walls, has quite an advantage over some less well-endowed town halls, and I would be inclined to check discreetly what sort of reception might be on offer before you apply. It is also worth trying to instigate hospitality from City companies, commercial or industrial concerns and other well-funded bodies that are related to your organisation or that see your delegates as suitable targets for publicity or you as a worthy cause. Two of the most glamorous conference entertainments I've ever experienced fell into this category: a reception at the Goldsmiths' Hall on Aslib's 50th Anniversary and a soirée in Elsevier's fabulous premises (with fabulous food and drink) in Amsterdam.

Getting off to a good start. . .
Left to yourself and your budget there are possibilities enough. The social programme is supposed to be fun – well, I don't know if it is always that, but at least it can be well arranged. More important than originality or lavishness is a good match to your audience – don't have a wine tasting at a temperance conference, for instance (though for a different public a wine tasting can be very good fun). It is difficult to go wrong with food and drink and, however unambitious, I think the first evening of your event should include a social get-together, with drinks and some attempt by the organisers to effect introductions, to draw the obvious loners into groups. Conferences are often launched by a keynote address in the auditorium on the

first evening; if you don't decide on this, what about some sort of feature at the first dinner – at least a short welcoming speech from the chair or president? Or you may reserve this formal welcome for the drinks reception after dinner. If you have an exhibition running concurrently with your conference, an ideal opportunity to launch this and make sure that delegates have a chance to see it and meet the exhibitors is just such a welcome reception on the first evening: the exhibits, the need to move around, looking and asking questions, are themselves useful means of breaking down shyness and inhibitions. When delegates first arrive they are still more than half in their own worlds; nothing too hearty or involving too much participation is welcome, and the exhibition may be an effective way of easing them into the conference theme.

As every host or hostess knows, small numbers make for easier and more relaxed socialising. In a really small gathering, a get-together after dinner in a common room with drinks and perhaps everyone asked to introduce themselves and say why they are there could be a good opening gambit. As always, the gregarious and those already acquainted go off together and it is to take care of the quite large number who are not immediately confident and outgoing that a constant supply of social events is needed.

. . . and keeping it up

I think every evening of the conference should offer something, but you should not necessarily expect that everyone will take up your offer. This can tax your invention a little, but what about a film show, or the chance to visit the local theatre (but I haven't generally noticed much enthusiasm for this)? Many places are well provided with local attractions and some delegates are happy to be 'free in . . .' as the tour operators say. If you have opted for a civic reception this could well be on your second night, and the so-called conference banquet generally occupies the final evening. This event, in one form or another, is now almost *de rigueur* – it may be just a slightly better dinner than usual in your conference hotel or hall of residence, or you may decide to lash out, or move to different and more exciting surroundings. Whatever you do, be sure to decide before your conference budget is finalised.

Wherever you hold your banquet, you'll want to arrange the room to give it a sense of occasion. Perhaps you want a top table and formal seating, though for pleasure and conviviality I recommend tables for eight or ten, space permitting. You will in any case expect sparkling glass and linen, flowers, silver, lights and, of course, a special menu. Such a dinner needs to be preceded by a drinks reception, ideally in an adjoining room; dinner should be formally announced and the diners move simultaneously to their places at this signal. If you have a top table, you'll undoubtedly have a table plan, and those seated at the top table need to be alerted beforehand – indeed, they may be segregated in a separate, smaller reception from which, when the rest of the delegates are seated, they are ushered out to take their places. Some people dislike this formality, or find it ridiculous – it is all a matter of taste and you will do what you think or your committee wants, or what is your organisation's normal practice. If you are having speeches, don't forget the microphone. And you would do well to employ a toastmaster. These gentlemen are often town hall officials (past or present), they have stentorian voices, a grand manner (and often rather colourful dress) and sometimes a profound knowledge of precedence, which can be useful on occasion. If you have a table plan for the whole company (quite a formidable task for you) this should be displayed and additional copies given to the diners as they arrive at the pre-banquet reception.

Speeches do almost always seem to crop up at conference banquets – they can be a bonus or a bore. If there is a series of toasts and thank-yous the maxim is, keep them short (speakers should, of course, have been briefed in advance). If you invite after-dinner speakers for their entertainment value, make sure they are entertaining or have something really worth saying that they say well. A flightier alternative to a speaker would be a cabaret or floor show. Here I will confine myself to saying, consider your audience's likely reaction and don't forget the cost. If you are using a hotel, you may have thought of turning your banquet into a dinner dance, but stop a moment: how about the male/female ratio, are numbers fairly evenly matched? This matters less if instead you provide a disco – wallflowers and those who can't face the hurly-burly and the din can retire to a lounge or the bar without loss of face.

A move out of the conference hotel or residence may make your banquet more of an occasion, especially if you are using institutional accommodation, however good. The justification for this, of course, must be a really good dinner in a setting that is unusual, beautiful or memorable in its own right. This is where dinner on a riverboat might come in, in Whitehall Palace, a livery company hall (some are available, such as the Cutlers' Hall in Sheffield), while many stately homes now offer banqueting facilities. Your source of information for this will be the local tourist office, who will also tell you to whom application should be made.

Many social events that take you away from your conference base mean transport and, even if your delegates are not all staying at the conference hotel or residence, this should at least be considered; for a residential conference all housed in the same place it almost always applies. To leave people in a strange city to find their own way for any distance is asking for problems, late arrivals and general dissatisfaction. So when you book the facility, make sure you also book the bus transport, not forgetting to count the cost.

As well as contributing greatly to delegates' enjoyment and their chances of meeting each other, the social programme is an opportunity to thank benefactors – sponsors, the city (if there has been a civic reception), chairs, speakers, the committee; and to entertain any influential people whose interest and support you would like to enlist. I think a really well developed social sense (which is what you need here) is quite rare and you, as conference organiser, will be too busy to do much more than set up the conditions in which your chair and other leading members of your organisation can operate. Somehow you must activate them, not only to talk to the Lord Mayor (who incidentally has to be met on the doorstep and led to the reception room) or your guest of honour, but to make sure that they are at all times circulating happily, talking to someone. And then of course there are your speakers, possibly guests from overseas and those who are meeting your organisation for the first time. I think members of your committee should have specific tasks here, to take care of such categories of delegate or guest, to make sure they feel welcome and are integrated into the proceedings as a whole. In a small conference all this happens quite easily, but with large numbers you have to work hard at the human side as well as coping with the organisation – getting people on and off buses, obviating queues for cloakrooms, ensuring that the whole of the civic reception isn't spent waiting to shake hands with the Mayor.

Out and about – the visits programme

Rather similar feats of organisation are involved in your visits programme and here too some sponsorship may be involved. The visits can be very much integrated into your conference and a serious contribution to its theme, or they can be peripheral – a junket or an 'accompanying person's programme', which needs rather a different approach, in my view.

A good programme of visits is undoubtedly quite a draw, but if you are selling a serious and hardworking conference to busy and expensive people (whose fees will be paid by their employers) the visits need to look relevant to their speciality and the conference theme, and preferably be something that is not too readily on view. You may have chosen the location of your conference with some particular site or installation that you want to examine in mind, but if not, you will have to draw on the advice of local specialists in your subject – one or two of whom you will hope to have recruited to your committee. (For an archaeological conference, for instance, local archaeologists should put you wise to what is worth a visit in the area and should have the *entrée* to sites not open to the general public. Local pharmaceutical companies might well welcome a visit from a conference of pharmacists.) You will also want to show your delegates some of the characteristic features of the neighbourhood you have chosen, and this could mean its industry, landscape, notable institutions or buildings. Inevitably, tourism will creep in and you will certainly find the local tourist office a useful source of ideas. They should also be able to advise you about the bus transport you will need to hire.

Having negotiated your various visits – date, time, duration, number in the party – you will approach the coach operator for a quotation. With this and any costs of the visits themselves, such as entrance fees, guides, tips to drivers and such contingencies, you will be able to cost your visits programme – a cost which will be included in the conference fee. When publicising the conference, I suggest you ask delegates to indicate the visit of their choice with their registration. Although much subsequent chopping and changing is likely to occur, this at least gives you an idea of how support for the various visits is going, enabling you to make any necessary modifications in the arrangements. At the conference itself the lists of participants in each visit should be displayed and at the appropriate time and place you will have the task of shepherding your delegates onto their correct buses. You can imagine a scene of chaos here (if you haven't ever been part of one): queues forming, people rushing from one to another, buses delayed (in fact, they often have to arrive in sequence, rather than all being drawn up in one place). You can help yourself and them by providing the buses in advance with large notices stating their destination. You – and any assistants you can muster from your staff – will have to urge and direct the travellers onto their buses and wave them away when the load is complete. (A loud-hailer is invaluable here!) Transport is always one of the frailer links in the organisational chain. You are painfully dependent on your coach operator and the competence of his or her employees, so choose one carefully and don't always go for the lowest bidder. Very full and careful briefing and keeping in constant touch, with a bit of luck, can generally ensure that all goes reasonably well.

It is important to have a leader for each of your coach parties (possibly drawn from your staff or committee). This person has at the least the responsibility for counting heads on and off the bus and making sure no one is left behind on the return journey. If there is an entrance fee to pay, he or she should be entrusted with the necessary funds. If you are being received as guests he or she should thank the hosts for their welcome. On tourist visits particularly it is very well worth going to the extra trouble and expense of securing a guide, who can provide background information and in general greatly enhance the interest of the tour; and I think that for visits to industrial plants or institutions this too could apply – possibly the leader you have recruited could be briefed to tell the party a little about the context of their visit before they arrive.

There can be a slight variation on this scenario in the case of a major national or international conference or when a prestigious foreign association, such as the American Bar Association, meets in the UK. Then it is likely that hospitality and tours will be offered, perhaps on quite a large scale, the expenses being borne by the hosts. Your role then as organiser would probably be confined to handling the bookings and laying on and paying for the transport – a co-operative effort where it is very important to know from the outset exactly what your responsibilities are.

'Extracurricular' visits
It is for such large and generally up-market conferences that the so-called 'accompanying person's programme' is needed. This assumes that many or most of your delegates are accompanied by a husband, wife, child, lover or other hanger-on, not participating in the conference, for whom a programme of visits and other events has to be provided. A number of points need to be established at the outset: is it likely (have you a precedent?) that most of your accompanying persons will want to join the visits that you offer? With a limited and fairly homogeneous group, or if you are in a foreign country, it is likely that most will; with a larger group on more familiar ground it is less likely. Who is going to pay? Should the cost be included in the conference budget and covered by the delegates' fees, or will the programme be an extra, paid for as it is taken up? The former is quite an extravagant option but the easiest to operate. The latter could lead to a great deal of unproductive paperwork in the way of invoicing (and some loss of support) and possibly not enough saving to offset the aggravation involved.

Here you will be laying on visits with a tourist flavour – for instance, visits to stately homes, to gardens, a porcelain factory, a silversmith or jeweller, a fashion show, a wildlife park, a football match, or a race meeting. Originality, exclusivity, attention to comfort are qualities to aim for here; inside information and personal contacts are the best recipe for this, and if you can hand the whole programme over to an operator with this expertise I would do so.

At a less ambitious level, you may not be providing a visits programme either as part of the conference or for accompanying persons, but wish to make it easy for delegates, in their spare time, or for those accompanying them to enjoy the attractions of the neighbourhood. Here you can generally enlist local help –

the tourist office will certainly give you information and a local tour operator might be willing to set up a desk in your conference complex. If he or she will give you material to distribute in advance, some tours could be pre-booked, or you may be able to persuade him or her to put on one or two tours specially for your delegates at his or her own risk. Your conference centre may offer tourist information and handle bookings; it also may have its own leisure facilities, such as swimming pool, sauna, tennis courts and golf. Publicise these: along with the activities and distractions you have organised they can give your conference the added zest and sense of occasion that is one of the hallmarks of success.

C H A P T E R   8

Keeping the record and keeping in touch

This chapter is concerned with an important but unsung aspect of organising your conference – recording, informing and keeping in touch. Much of what I have to say may seem obvious and is intended mainly as an *aide mémoire*, while some of my suggestions for devising a set formula and standardised letters may avoid confusion and omissions and lighten your workload.

Keeping in with the place

Your first contact will be with your location – university, conference centre and/or hotel. Your inspection and discussions have finally resulted in a firm booking and a contract, in which exactly what you are hiring, under what conditions and at what price are clearly stated and agreed. This may be many months before the event and it is hardly likely that you will not need to be in touch again. Subsequent developments may mean minor adjustments to the arrangements and these should all be carefully recorded in writing. The publication of your main publicity material is an opportunity to keep your conference in mind by sending the programme with a brief covering note: 'You will be interested to see the programme of our conference . . . I will be in touch about details nearer the time.'

'Nearer the time' will probably be about three or four weeks before the event, when the documentation for delegates should be ready and distributed. It is advisable to send a set of these documents to the conference manager at your location. The most important of these will, of course, be the detailed programme giving the place and times of registration, catering, sessions and social and other events. The programme should be accompanied by a catering brief, with times of meals, teas and

coffees and bar openings; and a brief for the projection department stating what public address and projection facilities are
needed and at what times and when a projectionist is required.
By some date specified by the location you will have to provide
the list of those to be accommodated (if yours is a residential
conference) and the catering numbers for each meal. I need
hardly say that for a one-day conference this is simply the
number of delegates attending. For a longer conference you may
have variations in attendance from day to day, and for a residential conference the same applies: some of your delegates may not
stay the whole course, may opt out of the banquet, etc. (and you
may have guests at the banquet), so you should at least consider
doing an individual count for each meal. (Specimen formats for
these briefs are at Appendices 9 and 10.)

Speakers – persuading, reminding, keeping

Your initial approach to speakers is a very individual affair – by
telephone, by letter, using a mutual friend as an intermediary –
and as for methods of persuading, you are probably far more
adept than I! But at some point you must issue a formal letter of
invitation, which should, of course, provide the vital information about the conference: date, place, theme, object, those it is
likely to attract and the numbers you expect. The invitation to
contribute a particular paper should specify the duration of the
paper, whether it will be published – and if so, when the text
will be required – and finally state the conditions of the
invitation: if you are offering a fee, meeting travel expenses,
offering free attendance at the conference. Finally, include a
sentence saying how delighted/honoured and so forth you
would be by their acceptance and hoping to hear from them
soon. Obviously you will be writing a great many very similar
letters, so it is worth drafting this invitation so that all but the
paragraph asking for a specific contribution can be standardised
(see Appendix 11). Then if you have a word processor you are
well away and even if each letter has to be typed individually you
can save yourself drafting and dictating time. Don't, however, be
tempted into using an obviously reproduced letter topped and
tailed and with insertions. The individual approach is very
important indeed. Unfortunately, your invitations may languish
unanswered and you'll have to send chasers; here I don't recommend standard letters so much as telexes and telephone calls.

It goes without saying that acceptances should be briefly and gratefully acknowledged, with the promise to be in touch again; and the moment for this will be when the programme and registration form are issued – about six months, or possibly a good deal less, before the date of the conference. I've talked about this letter to speakers and the accompanying notes about presentation, audiovisual facilities and so forth in my chapter 'Putting on the show', and a specimen text is at Appendix 8. This is a very important communication – it enables you to brief your speakers in as much detail as you decently can. The form you ask them to return should give you the material about them and their papers for the programme handbook and proceedings, and tell you what accommodation and other facilities they will need. Here I recommend a quite brief personal letter (which can be standardised, however) and your more general note (Appendix 8). You are likely to have to chase after this information, but as it reminds your speakers of their commitment to you perhaps that's no bad thing. Your final communication will be three or four weeks before the conference, when documents for all the delegates go out. This communication will include the final version of the programme or programme handbook, however you describe it, with a list of delegates attending, any information you decide to issue about the place (how to get there and so forth), invitation cards for any social events, a form for return to you claiming travel and other expenses, and a personal letter stating what accommodation and other arrangements you have made for their stay. If you have planned a briefing meeting for speakers and chairs at the conference – and I do urge this – now is the moment to tell them of it. No other communication will be as effective as this – to make sure they're there, that they know how the sessions are organised, that the chairs have read their speakers' biographies, that you've been told about all the audiovisual facilities needed. I think this personal letter is important – form letters are so often not read.

Keeping track of the transport
If you are planning a visits programme you will have been in touch with your potential hosts at a fairly early stage and, having secured them, you will have approached the local coach

operator with a detailed specification of your transport needs, on which his or her estimate will be based. It is courteous as well as advisable to remind both your hosts and the coach operator of your existence by sending them a copy of your programme when it is issued. Shortly before the event you should write with the final programme and any up-dating of the arrangements that are necessary – revision of numbers, for instance – and lists of those participating in the visits to the various hosts. In a previous chapter I mentioned the provision of large labels showing the destination of visits for display in the buses (your organisation's name is enough if buses are meeting delegates at the railway station): immediately before the conference you should arrange to meet the coach operator's controller of your transport to hand over these labels and make sure that all the arrangements are well in hand. It is essential that you have his or her telephone number at all times in case any snags develop.

The delegates – registering and recording
From soon after the distribution of your programme, bookings for your conference will be coming in. They must be acknowledged, either with a receipt for the money enclosed or an invoice for the fee; and you may accompany this by a form letter (as at Appendix 12), mentioning, for instance, that a handbook will be published shortly before the event, when details of accommodation and joining instructions will be given, warning perhaps that payment should be made before these items can be issued, giving information about any special offers, such as British Rail's concessionary fare, the travel agent who can deal with hotel bookings, and so forth.

Keeping the record
You also have the task of filing these applications in the most practical way for your purposes. You have designed your registration form (see Appendix 4) to give you the information you need to keep in touch, to invoice and list your delegates and to tell you exactly what they have booked for. This includes name, title, organisation, address; whether residential (and if so for how many nights) or non-residential; what receptions or other special features – such as visits – they have opted for; how

they are travelling – rail, road, air – if this is relevant to your arrangements. If this record is kept manually, you have the option of filing alphabetically under organisation (in which case you have everyone from the same organisation together) or under surnames. I think you will have no difficulty in deciding which listing to employ: if you are an organisation with personal members, obviously you will go for names; if you have corporate membership, the organisations that are members should be listed. If your conference is not aimed at a particular membership organisation, I would suggest listing under names, though delegates' affiliations should probably appear. Ideally, a list of those attending should be included with the documents mailed shortly before the conference (as delegates appreciate a preview of who they will be meeting) with an up-dated list given to them on arrival at the conference. The second of the two lists needs to include not only the organisation but the full address.

If you are able to use a computer to record your registrations you are at an enormous advantage, with a number of labour-saving devices to hand. As you set up your program, think of the categories you would like to be able to pick out: obviously names (alphabetically) and organisations (alphabetically), both with addresses; residential or non-residential; attending which receptions or visits; regional perhaps – northern, midland, metropolitan, overseas; how travelling; whether paid on application or invoiced, and when paid. The first and most obvious advantage of this computerised list of registrations is that it can be printed out for mailing documents to delegates and to furnish your attendance list, which can then be reproduced in the necessary numbers, saving a big typing load; and it can be constantly brought up to date. It is also valuable in keeping track of the receipt of conference fees and can be programmed to invoice for outstanding payments.

Joining instructions – the 'final' documents

By now you will have gathered that the big moment for communication is three to four weeks before the conference (less if you're working to a briefer timescale), when documents and joining instructions are mailed to the delegates. Of course, the most important of these is the final programme or handbook, whichever you call it. This can be a simple leaflet or almost a small book, containing not only the detailed programme with abstracts of the papers, but biographies of the speakers, descriptions of visits and also of any supporting exhibition, with write-ups of the exhibits. In addition, there must be all the necessary joining instructions and information about the location, social events and other arrangements. A visit to your location, to remind yourself of the details of these arrangements, may be advisable before you go to press. Bear in mind that such a volume will be a significant item in your budget and will take some time to produce – you would be wise to allow about ten weeks from the day you give the copy to the printer to publication. I've suggested in a previous chapter that the design of this handbook should be *en suite* with the rest of your printed matter and that you may also be able to sell advertisement space to meet some of your printing costs.

Whatever the scope of this document, its basic contents must include the finalised programme with titles of papers and names of speakers; times and place of the sessions; directions for arrival and registration – when and where; details of accommodation, of social events and catering – with times; if you are using a university, a plan of the conference area is advisable, showing lecture area, refectory, halls of residence; a map showing approaches to the centre, parking facilities and so forth are invaluable additions. Although your handbook may go into considerable detail about the various arrangements for delegates, if they are at all complicated or varied, and particularly if you are handling room bookings, as in a university, I would recommend a duplicated letter (see Appendix 13) in which you fill in the individual arrangements you have made for each delegate while reiterating the general information in the programme – which very probably won't be read.

Supplementing this programme handbook, you will probably decide to send a list of those attending, with any tickets or invitations. If you have any not too bulky information about your conference centre and a map, these might usefully be included. This, too, is the moment to despatch preprints, if they are being produced.

The whole issue of preprints is, in my view, open to debate. They presuppose that the texts will be studied in advance and that the papers will be commentaries on these texts, which are then thrown open to discussion. If your programme demands this format, your speakers must be told well in advance (in fact, when they're invited) and you must undertake the collection, reproduction and mailing of the texts – a big task. Although delegates like texts – as a proof they've been to the conference and to save them the bother of taking notes – I cannot believe there is much point in them unless they are received in advance; to provide them on the day simply ensures a rustle of turning pages as the speaker talks, and is a temptation not to attend the sesssion at all.

On site on the day
Much of the ease and smooth running of your conference will depend on the communication network you've been able to set up at your location. As soon as you arrive, make contact with the centre's manager, run through all the arrangements with him or her and make sure you know on whom to call for last-minute adjustments or if problems arise. You should know how to reach the projection department, the caterer, where to turn if you need a doctor, an extra blanket, a special diet, a taxi, travel information. Set up your conference office, which ideally should immediately adjoin the conference desk (of which more anon), check the telephone, arrange to meet the controller of your transport. As far as possible, make sure you know your way around the location itself.

The first contact with delegates at the place on the day may be your signposting. In the UK you can often commission the AA or RAC to provide this for you, and some conference-conscious cities do it themselves – and very pleasant that is: I remember how my heart lifted driving up the autobahn from Munich airport to see the name of my conference prominently displayed. If you are providing transport to meet delegates at the airport or railway station, make sure that the name of your conference is displayed on the bus. At the location itself at least the entrance should be marked and, if your activities extend over a large area, the more signposting you can persuade your hosts to provide or you can set up yourself the better, to overcome the sense of disorientation that newly arrived delegates so often feel.

Above all, the registration area itself should be very clearly indicated and the greatest trouble taken to avoid confusion or delays. Your badges and documents should, of course, be arranged alphabetically; break the alphabet into sections as appropriate – A – E, F – K, L – Q, R – Z – clearly marked, with a member of staff for each section, to minimise queueing. If you are expecting any problem registrants – for instance, new applicants, delegates paying their fees, for which receipts will have to be issued – it may be advisable to direct them to a separate point rather than hold up the movement of regular registrants. For a residential conference, checking into accommodation may coincide with registration itself. A hotel will have its routine and should be able to handle luggage and direct arrivals swiftly to their rooms. In a university you will find that practice varies. Room keys will be issued against a rooming list – yours as it stands or one made by the warden from your list. They often have to be signed for, which makes for delay, but sometimes you may be given the room numbers and keys and allowed to issue them when you hand out the documents. It is important to help delegates with their luggage and to find their rooms. You may have spare staff on hand who can do this, but better still, hire student help – often available – as they are familiar with the place, which your staff cannot possibly be.

The conference pack
The documents you offer at this point can be fairly meagre, or you may find yourself handing out quite a conference pack in a specially provided wallet. Absolutely basic is the badge, which delegates are urged to wear for the duration of the conference. Any supplier of conference materials will offer quite a choice of these; probably the most used and most popular is the plastic holder on a safety pin, into which a specially prepared card (usually sold in perforated strips) bearing the name can be inserted. These cards can be overprinted with the name or logo of your conference and the delegate's name will be typed on. Don't make the mistake of choosing badges that are too small. Lettering for the printed or typed name needs to be fairly large – say not less than 5mm in height – so that names can be read without peering too closely at your protagonist's bosom! (And

talking about personal labelling, on a much larger scale, don't forget the speakers' name cards for display on the platform that I mentioned in 'Putting on the show'.) Equally indispensable documents are the final list of those attending and any last-minute changes to the programme.

Other items you might include in your conference pack: cards for receptions, if you didn't mail them with the final pro-gramme; meal tickets or vouchers (if issued); a spare copy of the programme, if you're feeling generous (and anyway have a supply on hand for those who have forgotten their copies); any special notices about transport, the location of study groups and other arrangements; the banquet table plan, if you've prepared it in advance; texts of papers, if you didn't mail them with the documents as I suggested in a previous paragraph; tourist information about the locality; an order form for the proceedings or the proceedings themselves, if they are published in time for the conference and included in the package. This is your last opportunity to circularise the whole of your delegate body, so make the most of it. If you have to communicate with speakers or members of a special interest group, with instructions or invita-tions to a limited social function, this is the time to do so.

Contact on the ground

Keeping in touch with a large number of delegates throughout a conference is not always easy. You need to establish the confer-ence desk – which may not be where registration takes place – at the hub of the conference and at a point where it cannot be missed, and of course it should be staffed all the time. Here (or in the adjoining conference office – an extension would be ideal) you will have your telephone with the number that you have published as contact for the conference. The telephone is for your use and should definitely not be used by delegates for outgoing calls; but callers must be able to contact delegates on this number through you. To convey messages received nothing is as helpful as a public address system, enabling you to page delegates. Failing this, you will need to pin messages on the conference noticeboard; you may also resort to asking session chairs to announce that there are messages at the conference desk for named delegates. The conference noticeboard is impor-tant as a means of contact and communication; here you will display notices about transport, visits, announcements of developments in the programme or arrangements – all this in addition to the kind of 'interaction messaging' described in a previous chapter.

Another group of people may feel even more lost than your delegates – your guests. You've invited them, told them time and place. Make sure they know just where to come, which entrance to use, that there is someone to direct them to the cloakroom and finally to bring them to their host. The host also may need to be briefed.

Telling the home team

This brings me to the last but certainly not least important figure (I hope figures) to be kept thoroughly in the know: your staff and those of your committee – president, director, officers – who are actively involved in presiding over and hosting the conference.

I think by now you will have gathered that the flow of work on a conference is very uneven – sometimes hectic, sometimes comparatively quiet. A very few people can produce quite a large event, but when the day dawns and the delegates arrive you will find you need many hands at the pump. For a three- or four-day residential conference with 300–400 delegates I would recommend at least eight members of staff, who will be very well occupied, particularly if the sessions are rapporteured. And these staff members need to know just what they're about. If you have a large conference department with all members involved in the arrangements, to go through an annotated programme distributing the various jobs, and keeping a record of who is doing what, is probably enough. But if you are depending on the help of members of other departments, or if you have to recruit outside helpers, a detailed brief is essential. This brief – I have provided an example at Appendix 14 – is based on the detailed programme, with additions such as the arrival time of the president or VIPs, who may have to be met, when registration desks should be staffed, handouts distributed, speakers and projectionist brought together, lecture room set-up checked, with a note to whom these tasks have been assigned. Each staff member or helper should have a copy of this brief and if you can discuss the tasks with your helpers, either individually or all together, so much the better. I recommend a rendezvous first thing every morning in the conference office to check or modify these tasks.

Your chair may find it helpful to have a copy of this brief, but in any case you will need to make sure he or she knows exactly what has to be done and where to be at any given time. For instance, when and where he or she will be receiving guests and about the guests themselves. When it comes to speeches, be sure the chair knows who to thank. Helping him or her to adumbrate the conclusions of the conference and stage-managing the occasion when this is done may also fall to you.

These are just a few examples. In an eventful programme there can be many developments and you will often have to improvise, but the kind of structure of contacts and communication I've suggested should help you to keep control of events.

At Appendix 15 you will find a checklist of items mentioned in this chapter for 'keeping in touch'.

CHAPTER 9

The exhibition

Exhibitions, perhaps even more than conferences, are a growth industry, and this is reflected in the increasing number of conferences that are accompanied by an exhibition of some kind. I say 'some kind' because the so-called conference exhibition is often no more than a few tables, strategically placed, displaying leaflets about goods and services – perhaps the goods themselves, if the near certainty of their being stolen can be accepted. But these exhibitors are there because they see there is money in it for them, and, as it means some trouble and probably expense for you, there's every reason why there should be a little profit in it for you too. When these simple arrangements burgeon into something like fifty units of exhibition space, with stands, display panels, tables, lighting and telephones (though this is small beer compared with the big commercial exhibition), a considerable amount of money and professional skill is needed. What I can tell you won't qualify you for a job at Olympia, but it should introduce you to the basic principles of the art.

Delegates like exhibitions, but the paradox is that the exhibition to which you have given place is not only an added attraction but in some ways in competition with your conference, and the exhibitors will certainly feel that your sessions are in competition with them. So the first essential is to make sure that the exhibition is placed at the focal point of the conference, where delegates cannot fail to see it – and ideally are irresistibly drawn to it for other reasons, such as catering and the presence of bars – and that the programme allows them plenty of time to visit the stands and meet the exhibitors. If you can hold the welcome reception I have recommended for the first evening actually on the site of the exhibition, this both throws delegates and exhibitors together in a convivial way and makes

the opening of the exhibition a prominent feature of the programme. Incidentally, you may be able to persuade the exhibitors to meet the cost of the reception. Obviously, exhibitors
want as much exposure as possible: they see your delegates as
customers and, though it is often impracticable to open conference exhibitions to the general public, if you can in some way
give access to interested parties outside your delegate body, so
much the better.

The space and how it's used

An exhibition takes up a great deal of space – in Appendices
16a and 16b I show a couple of typical layouts, which occupy
about 7,500 and 5,400 square feet respectively. If, looking at
these plans, you think the space has been used extravagantly,
remember there must be access to all the stands for perhaps a
few hundred delegates, that there are doors and windows here
and there (and sometimes pillars, as in Appendix 16a), and that
the stands must on no account mask each other. When you
choose your exhibition site make very sure there is adequate
access. This is always important, but supremely so for a large
exhibition where stands have to be erected, and furniture and
possibly really large exhibits will have to be brought in. Access
doesn't just mean a large door and a large service lift but the
possibility of unloading large vehicles at the exhibition
entrance. As well as access there is the question of security –
despite my remarks about 'no responsibility' later in this chapter. With valuable exhibits this cannot be overlooked. Although
natural light for your site is a consideration, far more important
are power cables and the possibility of installing a large number
of thirteen-amp power points. It is quite common practice to
include one such power point and a 100-watt spotlight with
each stand. If your exhibitors are displaying electrical equipment they may need additional power. They may also need to
install one or more telephones, either for demonstration purposes or simply convenience. You must be sure all such facilities are available.

If you are thinking of the small, informal exhibition, without
built units – a table and perhaps a couple of chairs and some
additional lighting – you will need to mark out the area

allowed for each such simple set-up and its location on a scale plan of the room, which should also show doors and windows. Your conference centre may be able to provide suitable tables, tablecloths and chairs, either free or for a fee, or you may have to hire them from a contractor. A great addition to such a simple scheme would be a display panel behind the table. Some of your exhibitors may bring their own; if not, there is the possibility of hiring them from an exhibition contractor. But this, of course, is the beginning of the road to built stands.

Building the exhibition

The structure needed for your unit or stand is very simple – a back panel and two side partitions enclosing an area of space with, across the front, a fascia board to carry the exhibitor's name (see Appendix 17). There are many such systems and your choice will largely depend on what is provided by the exhibition contractor you employ. Needless to say, the choice of contractor is immensely important. Nothing can replace personal experience; failing this, seek really reliable advice, given with the knowledge of your particular situation and needs. Meet the contractor and, if possible, see his or her equipment in action, or at the very least illustrated. Prices can vary dramatically, so go for more than one estimate. Lists of exhibition contractors can be found in *The Exhibitors' Handbook* (Kogan Page Ltd).

To give a realistic estimate, the contractor will have to visit the site. I would recommend accompanying him or her at some point in the negotiations. With a scale plan of the area he or she will then produce a proposed layout for your exhibition. This scheme will most probably provide units of a standard size – I have found 8ft × 4ft (2.44m × 1.22m) convenient – and I recommend offering space only in units of the standard size. Your contractor should not only provide the stand units, transport, erect and dismantle them, but also provide the lettering for the exhibitors' names on the fascia boards and any electrical equipment, such as spotlights, and, in co-operation with the lessor of the space, undertake the necessary electrical work. It will be important, when he or she inspects the site, to make sure that the cabling is adequate for this. If there has to be extra cabling, you must keep track of the cost. In addition, each stand will need some simple furniture – a table and a chair or two; hanging shelves for display are also often in demand and you should be able to hire them from the contractor. For a big installation, a number of workers will be necessary and it is possible that some may have to be accommodated at some point. Make sure that all these items are included in the estimate you finally accept.

The cost

The costs of your exhibition include the overhead, to be calculated as I described in Chapter 4. In some ways, for an exhibition that is part of a conference, this can be seen as a somewhat notional figure, or just a share of the conference overhead. However, to arrive at a realistic unit cost, try to set an overhead additional to the figure for your conference. The contractor's charge for the provision and erection of stands I have described above. The hire of space may be quoted as a round sum or as a per-square-foot or square-metre figure. In either case, think of it as a total sum (as, however many stands you erect, you're likely to have to pay for the whole area) and the number of units you can sell bears no direct relation to the square footage.

Printing and publicity should not be a large item, as it will be largely subsumed in the conference publicity. Every leaflet, advertisement and press release should mention that there will be an exhibition: some at least will reach potential exhibitors. You will, however, need to print a prospectus (as at Appendix 18) for fairly limited distribution, and an exhibition handbook. The latter is important to the exhibitors, as it gives publicity to them and their products. If your printing schedule permits, I would recommend combining the exhibition handbook with the main handbook of the conference. Unless you can manage a very glossy exhibition handbook, this gives it more prestige than a smallish leaflet on its own. One final cost – the exhibitor's representative. It is usual to allow one per unit to attend the conference free, and the cost of this to you must be added to the unit cost. So your budget will look something like this:

	£
Overhead	000
Contractor's fee for building and transport of x stands, with fascia lettering, table, chair, one 13-amp point and spotlight	000
Hire of space	000
Printing and publicity	000
	0,000
Unit cost with one representative @ £y	0,000

$$\frac{0,000}{\text{number of units}} + £y$$

This figure is the unit cost to you (and the total cost of your exhibition is this sum multiplied by the number of units), but remember that the same uncertainty about numbers exists as for the conference itself. To ensure that you at least cover your costs, each unit should be charged at a figure noticeably in excess of this. Throughout all your costing operation, you need to have in mind the kind of price you think you can persuade your exhibitors to pay per unit (watch the market, ask your friends, even try out a price informally with one or two potential exhibitors you know). If you sell all your units you should budget for quite a nice profit. Otherwise, I cannot help feeling, the great additional hassle and expense of an exhibition has been in vain.

You'll notice I've suggested including the minimum standard items of furniture – table, chair, thirteen-amp power point, spotlight – in the charge for each unit of space, which can save everyone a lot of trouble. For extra items – more power points and/or spotlights, chairs, shelves, etc., exhibitors should be asked to apply to the contractor direct. If telephone facilities are needed, for online equipment or simply convenience, special application has to be made to the national telecommunications authority: your location will give details of whom to approach in the area. The full cost of these installations should be borne by the exhibitor. The exhibitor (not you) must make the application and the contract will be between him or her and the authority.

Selling the exhibition space

You will notice in my conference calendar (Appendix 1) that mailing the prospectus to exhibitors happens at about the same time as distribution of the main programme. This is not because the prospectus goes to the same people but because I believe that it is important to give the potential exhibitors as much information as possible about the conference. If you have already produced a call for papers or an attractive flyer, this would probably do as well.

The mailing list for your prospectus will comprise the producers of goods and services that your delegates are interested to see and likely to buy. (Incidentally, these are the people who might like to buy advertising space in your handbook or other publication, perhaps at a special rate for exhibitors.) You will need to study the classified lists of the industries concerned, while a few catalogues of exhibitions in your field would give you names and addresses and an idea of who are in the exhibiting business. The first time you launch an exhibition you can be very anxious, with no idea what the response will be. Once you are established the space can go very quickly. It is always wise to say in the prospectus that space is limited, as indeed it is. This can also be your excuse for a telephone follow-up, especially to old supporters or anyone you feel should be particularly interested, if demand seems to be flagging a bit. Meanwhile, of course, the rest of your conference publicity is keeping up the pressure.

The prospectus

At Appendix 18 you will see a specimen prospectus and space booking form. After the opening blurb, in which you need to stress the importance of the conference (and hence the exhibition), its theme and the range and number of delegates you expect, you should state as succinctly as possible the place of the exhibition in the conference complex and its relationship to the proceedings and facilities; how space is allotted; times of opening; access; cost; a date for the handbook copy; conditions of hire; and, most importantly, a plan of the exhibition area and form of application for space. The location may lay down further conditions that you must incorporate, but the conditions listed under 8 in the specimen prospectus are, in my view, the basic minimum for the efficient production of the exhibition and your protection. In respect of payment of the hire charge, you can and must be tough. Application for space should be made in writing, accompanied by a deposit of 50 per cent of the hire charge, the balance to be paid by a specified date, and failure to complete by that date giving you the right to reallocate the space, retaining the deposit. This, as you can imagine, discourages cancellation, and no refund of the deposit or hire charge need be offered in the event of cancellation. Keen exhibitors, or an exhibition that is known to be well supported, may mean some attempts to book by telephone. By all means pencil in the space and don't release it without reference to the applicant, but insist on written confirmation and the deposit. No booking should be treated as firm until these are received.

Conditions vii and viii under 8 in my prospectus emphasise the importance of insurance. You will already have insured your conference: to this should be added the maximum figure you could earn from the sale of exhibition space. At the same time, don't overlook the vital importance of the waiver of responsibility. 'The exhibitors exhibit entirely at their own risk.' You must disclaim liability for losses or damage to persons or property sustained by the exhibitors or their agents. Exhibitors should be strongly urged to insure against such contingencies and against the liability to indemnify the host conference (you) against liabilities, actions, costs, claims and compensation for injury or loss to any person or damage to or loss of any property.

Because so many different agencies are concerned – the conference centre, local suppliers and technicians, the exhibition contractor, possibly the national telecommunications authority, the exhibitors, who may be disorganised and dilatory – an exhibition offers plenty of opportunities for problems and disasters. Locations vary in efficiency and sophistication, and the quality of your contractor and his or her ability to deal with the location and the exhibitors are all-important. Never skimp on the time allowed for building the exhibition, even if it means the expense of an extra day's hire of the space. Draft your application form so that it provides the vital information: how the exhibitor's name should appear on the fascia, what extra equipment or facilities are needed. Pass these on to your contractor in good time. Set ample deadlines for applications for special facilities, particularly telephone installations; they won't be adhered to, but keep after them so that, on the day, everything does in fact come together as desired. You will in any case plan to arrive at the location twenty-four hours or so before the conference starts, and this is all the more desirable when an exhibition is involved. The sight of half-built stands and trailing wires is enough to strike gloom into any conference organiser's heart but, amazingly, by the deadline (exhibitors should have access to their stands to set up their exhibits about eight hours before the exhibition opens) all is generally in place. Take the opportunity to check the power points. These should be placed – one or more as ordered – in the individual units. Electricians must resist the temptation to install points in clusters, as this can give rise to heated arguments between exhibitors about which point belongs to whom, besides the obvious hazard of leads snaking their way around the stands. Erecting an exhibit can be quite testing for exhibitors themselves, in an unfamiliar setting, with the added hazard of bits of equipment or exhibits left behind or gone astray. If you can arrange for a bar with coffee, sandwiches and drinks to be open in the vicinity, this will be supportive, as will your presence on the scene.

Joining instructions

When the final documents are mailed to delegates you will also be mailing joining instructions to the exhibitors. These will be very similar to the set of documents going to delegates – the programme handbook; exhibition handbook, if it is not part of the main programme; attendance list (very important to exhibitors); any relevant tickets or invitations; a note about accommodation, if you've been asked to arrange it; and joining instructions. These should reiterate where the exhibition area can be entered, the time it will be open for the installation of exhibits and when they should be removed, along with any special instructions. The handbook, whether part of the main programme or a separate leaflet, should include a plan of the exhibition area with a list of exhibitors, indicating where on the plan they are placed. The descriptive notes about exhibitors will also show the stand number and may mention the names of the representatives in attendance.

Exhibitors' representatives

The exhibitors' representatives may add up to quite a high proportion of those attending the conference, if the exhibition is fairly large and the units are manned by more than one representative. It seems to me eminently reasonable that one representative should attend free of charge (i.e. actually paid for by the space hire) but as all exhibitors' representatives have exactly the same entitlement to sessions, catering, receptions, etc., as ordinary delegates there is no reason why their fee should be very noticeably less. Exhibitors' representatives are generally more volatile than delegates and you may have requests for one fee to cover a series of representatives, attending on consecutive days of the conference. All this involves more paperwork, amendments to lists and, of course, badges – and here at least you have people who are eager to be identified and who may even wear badges of their own. The badges that you issue should, of course, show name and company and be of some special design or colour to show their exhibitor status.

However well placed and well arranged your exhibition, it will only be judged a success if there are plenty of delegates and plenty of exposure for the exhibitors. An exhibition is certainly an added attraction but can hardly save a bad conference. A good reputation for either can have a snowballing effect. In this finely balanced interdependence can lie real enhancement of your conference, both as an event and in monetary terms.

CHAPTER 10

At the conference: an organiser's private view

On the eve

A couple of hours in the train and a chance to collect my wits and check my briefcase once more: copies of all the briefs, the master lists, files – accommodation, transport, speakers, exhibition, social. I forgot to put scissors and Blu-Tack on the packing list: let's hope Margot (my secretary) remembers.

A day of telephone calls while the final amendments to the attendance list roll off the printer and the cases are packed. One cancellation and one new booking – the cheque brought round by hand. Some anxious moments about Wednesday morning's opening speaker – a baggage handlers' strike at Charles de Gaulle Airport, but he's coming by train and ferry and will arrive late tomorrow night. As I leave the office, the minivan is delivered at the door. Our exhibition pack waiting in the hall, and two or three of the cases. The rest still to be packed and all to be loaded on the van this evening. Gerald and Margot and two others will start tomorrow morning at eight.

Arrive at our conference centre, notice a few – not enough – directional signs. No one much about. A message from the conference manager that he'll meet me at ten next morning. The usual sense of desolation, of a great space uninhabited, before the crowds and action begin. After drafting a few notices for the board, think of an early night but find two of our overseas delegates at the bar – they'd arrived on their Apex flight on Saturday and been here since last night. Do I think the heating could be turned up in their rooms? I am able to find them extra blankets and will talk to the manager about heating tomorrow.

The first day – all systems go!

Up betimes, breakfast from eight (it will be from seven-thirty for the rest of the conference). On my way to the dining room notice that the newsagent is already open and that the bank and post office are almost next door. Talk to the head porter at the reception desk about registration. He will set up tables where we can register delegates and hand out documents. He won't give me the room keys – these will be issued from his list in the porter's desk opposite. He swears it will go quite quickly – I only hope so. I should apply to him about any problems in the bedrooms – extra blankets or pillows, failed light bulbs, etc. The heating will be turned on full blast today.

With the conference manager, inspect the lecture theatre and main concourse. Erection of the exhibition is almost complete, spotlights going up and most of the fascia boards in place. Telephones not connected, however; I'm assured that the telephone engineers will be there before noon. Mid-morning the first of the exhibitors arrive. They brighten visibly when they see how close the bar is. I've arranged for them to lunch with my staff in the small dining room today.

The lecture theatre is as good as I'd first thought, and everything apparently in order. The two adjoining seminar rooms for the parallel sessions have been arranged, with classroom-style seating, overhead projectors and blackboards. I complain about insufficient signposting and succeed in persuading the conference manager (all jolly reassurance) that a few more notices are necessary. He's given me an extension on which he or his deputy can be reached at any time. The catering manager wants a word about the welcome reception – this will take place in the main concourse, amongst the exhibition. We'll walk through the foyer from the lecture theatre, so he'll set up tables with drinks that we'll pass as we enter the concourse. There will also be waitresses with trays. We don't plan a receiving line, but at some point the director may make a few welcoming remarks. I've asked for a microphone in case.

Soon after midday Gerald and Margot arrive with the van. Gerald and the other two begin to erect our exhibit. Margot and I unpack cases and set up the conference desk in the foyer outside the lecture theatre and the office in a little room, pokey but conveniently close. (We shall hardly use it, but it's useful to

have a bolthole and somewhere we can lock. The desk telephone can be unplugged and put there when there's no one on
the desk.) An excellent expanse of board for notices – we pin
up the announcements and lists.

After lunch the man from the bus company. We run through
the brief – no changes – and I give him the large destination
labels for the buses. Gerald will meet the buses at the railway
station this afternoon, to shepherd the arriving delegates on
board.

Registration due to start at four-thirty, so we'd better be ready
an hour before. Badges and conference packs arranged alphabetically; with 200–300 arriving in so short a time we'd better
have three streams, labelled A–G, etc. Margot, who has
handled registration and invoicing, will deal with any problem
arrivals. The conference pack includes an order form for the
proceedings, but I don't expect payment for this till later in the
conference. The first arrivals (car-borne) appear soon after
three. The head porter directs them to their rooms and whistles
up the rest of his staff. Soon after four-thirty the first busload
from the station, and after that a steady stream. Handing out the
documents goes smoothly, signing for room keys does cause a
slight bottleneck, as I'd feared, and a few ungracious grumbles.
The head porter calls in an assistant, which helps this. Staff are
there to assist with luggage and guide to rooms. You'd think
some people had come for a month, their cases are so numerous
and so bulging. One of our speakers has left his briefcase (with
his paper and slides) on the bus (thank God, not the train!). After
some frantic telephoning it is located and will be brought back
in the morning.

Dinner from six, a buffet, to cater for late arrivals. Registration desk open till eight. We take it in turns to staff it. Only a
trickle the last hour. After that the porter at the desk can hand
out room keys; documents can be collected next day at the
conference reception desk.

At seven-thirty I manage to collect most of the speakers at the
lecture theatre, with the projectionist, to test the facilities and
check the visual aids. We agree on the arrangement of the
platform and I have a quick recheck with my lecture-theatre staff
about passing the roving microphones, changing the speakers'
name cards and keeping the water carafe replenished (they

know, of course, I'll be around to back them up on these chores). One of the sessions will need two projectors – agree on their position now and also try out the placing of the overhead projector. Some of the overhead transparencies not all I could wish, but not much to be done at this stage. The opening session and keynote address get off almost on time with almost everyone there.

At the end of the session, my director leads the speaker straight through the foyer to the main concourse, thus setting the course for the welcome reception and the exhibition. Some of the exhibitors have already buttonholed waitresses to hover near their stands, thus ensuring circulation round the exhibits. Bar extension till midnight, so the drinking and talking go on quite late. I wait till my speaker off the Paris ferry arrives. He has dined on the train. Give him a drink and show him his room.

The second day – full steam ahead

By ten to eight, queues for breakfast – you'd think there was a risk of the cornflakes running out! Waylaid by one or two late arrivals, wondering where to pick up their conference wallets. Direct them to the conference reception desk, which opens at eight-thirty. The chair and all speakers for the first session collect in the lecture theatre by nine, projectionist arrives panting five minutes late. Remember to jot down the 'domestic' points I want the chair to make before the session breaks up – how long the coffee break will be and where, that messages will be displayed on the noticeboard behind the reception desk, where also mail for delegates will be. See the session start – a good chair, tells the audience just how he'll handle the discussion and that they must speak up (actually they'll be given roving mikes); introduces the speaker and his subject in a couple of witty sentences.

The bus operator comes with the forgotten briefcase – take the opportunity to re-schedule our return from the Assembly Rooms tonight – half an hour later for the last bus.

Visit the exhibition. Exhibitors seem happy with the opening and reception last night. They hope for more visitors this afternoon, during the parallel sessions. Some anxious questions about security this evening, when all delegates and exhibitors will be at the civic reception. Call up the conference manager, who assures us there have never been problems – they have a staff member patrolling and the concourse is locked at midnight. But if we would forego the bar after the reception, the area could be locked when we go in to dinner. Though some dedicated drinkers will no doubt still be thirsty at eleven-thirty, this seems the best compromise.

Coffee break approaching so check that the session is ending before alerting the caterer. For a few minutes the queue seems endless, but once the second point is sighted the service is very quick. Exhibitors all perking up and their stands soon full of activity. Just as well we've allowed fairly ample breaks between sessions. Manage to grab hold of the chair and ask him to announce the time and departure point for buses to the Assembly Rooms tonight. Will display large notice on the board with the same information.

A call from the City Hall about arrangements for this evening. The president and director to arrive ten minutes early by the private entrance for a drink with the Lord Mayor. No receiving line, I'm glad to say, just a few introductions of prominent members, speakers and guests. There will be a 'collation' and a few words of welcome by the Lord Mayor. They would like the president to reply. Have a word with the director about this – he will meet the president's train this afternoon and brief him about the reply. He asks me to list the thank-yous for the banquet tomorrow, which of course I do.

As expected, the parallel sessions in the afternoon provide an opportunity for some delegates to opt out – quite a number to the exhibition. One or two demonstrations are being staged. Despite this, both sessions are well attended, one to the extent of overcrowding. One never can tell how the interest will divide.

The president arrives soon after tea – says his wife would like to come for the banquet tomorrow if that could be arranged. No problem, his suite is a double.

Some scampering about after dinner, getting everyone on to the buses. Gerald and the rest very supportive, rounding up the stragglers while I go ahead with the director and president.

The Assembly Rooms, all white and gold with twinkling chandeliers, look wonderful. Very quick and efficient cloakrooms. The party streams up the wide, red-carpeted stairs to the parquet-floored ballroom. The 'collation' is of tremendous munificence – no need to have dined – which doesn't prevent the delegates falling on it like hungry wolves! Mercifully short speeches and then with a call, 'on with the revels', from the Lord Mayor, a band appears and dancing begins. One of the best civic receptions I've ever seen – and no one lost on the way home.

The third day – variations on a theme
I spoke too soon – there was a casualty last night. Carol B— slipped in 'Strip the willow' and turned her ankle. It's like a balloon this morning and can bear no weight. When Margot heard she'd missed breakfast she offered to take her tea and toast in her room. I called the local doctor who recommended the casualty department at the hospital for an X-ray. Borrowed the director's car to take her and Margot went as I couldn't leave the desk. Before lunch the visits stewards call in for lists and their briefs. Sooner than I'd dared hope, Margot brings Carol back – no break but she's well and truly strapped up and with a crutch. Proposing an afternoon on her bed but not missing the banquet.

Rush from dining room to the bus park to speed the visits buses on their way. Three already there, destination labels well displayed, the rest moving slowly up the drive. Delegates milling around, stewards waving their lists. I borrow a loud hailer and call out directions – I suppose the bus labels help but people don't seem to notice them much. Everyone on board at last and leaving with waves and smiles like a Sunday-school treat.

Agree the plan for the top table with the director. Margot types and duplicates this and types the place cards. Give the menus to the catering manager – and also the absolutely final numbers – and look over his arrangement of the tables: top table of twenty and small tables for ten. He is making the room look very nice, with candles and beautiful flowers. Pre-dinner reception is in the large foyer outside the dining room. We are serving sherry but the bar will also be open. A small anteroom off the dining room does very nicely for the director's reception for the top table guests. A call from the City Hall checking the time and reminding me that the Lord Mayor should be met at the front door on arrival. I tell them ten or soon after for the car to pick him up.

The place comes to life as the visits buses return – a rush for drinks as soon as the bars open, and for baths. The busload from the safari park very much delayed – half the party got lost and was three quarters of an hour late at the rendezvous (anxious moments wondering if they've had an encounter with the lions!). Time for a quick change before setting out the place cards on the top table. The toastmaster arrives and I brief him. I can see he's the managing type but luckily he doesn't argue with the ranking of the guests on the top table – obviously the Lord Mayor is the guest of honour – and he will certainly be helpful in getting the diners in and the guests placed.

The delegates' reception starts on the dot – in fact, quite a few arrive early, as always. I suppose they forget what agony it is for the hostess when guests arrive too soon. The president and director in the anteroom five minutes before the Lord Mayor due, joined by some of our keynote speakers and overseas guests. Meet the Lord Mayor at the main entrance and conduct him to the anteroom; the rest of the outside guests find their way unaided. The toastmaster announces dinner and the delegates pour in to take their places – I hope happily with their friends. He then lines up the top table guests so that they proceed automatically to their correct places. This always seems a bit pompous and ridiculous and gives rise to the odd crack, but it actually works well and avoids confusion. I head him off announcing grace, but he has his moment after dinner introducing the toasts, the speakers and the president, with a reply by the Lord Mayor. We forgot to test the microphone, but luckily it is switched on and works. We took a lot of trouble over the dinner menu, and didn't cut the cost, and I think it is really good and the service excellent. The bar is open in the main concourse till midnight, so the exhibitors that aren't more frivolously engaged have a final fling (they pack up in the morning). Well out of hearing there is a bar and disco for those more energetically inclined. A few private parties also seem to get going and I gather go on till far into the night.

The last day – thank you and goodbye
A sense of the morning after, and I guess some thick heads! Announcements about departure arrangements on the notice-board first thing – despite which a rush of enquiries about train

times, etc. We are providing buses to the station immediately after lunch and ordering taxis for those who must leave before this. However, an excellent final session should keep most delegates to the end. To reinforce this, ask the session chair to announce all these arrangements again and also to remind delegates that they can order the proceedings at a special rate, with a discount if they pay on ordering today. This produces a big spate of cash orders during the coffee break. Also manage during the morning to see almost all our speakers (two left yesterday) to thank them and, where possible, collect the texts of their papers. Take the opportunity to remind them to let me have their claims for expenses: one or two have already landed up on the desk. We decided to do a market survey on the conference – the questionnaire was in the conference packs – and a few are now handed in. Remember to ask the chair to mention this in his final address. The last few minutes devoted to thanks, some of it reiterating last night's speeches. I am glad that the arrangements at the centre are singled out for praise and that there is a kindly mention of the staff. Most of the delegates who say goodbye to me seem to have been happy – I hope we get a good press.

A great sense of anticlimax as the last bus leaves for the station. Our exhibit has been dismantled during the morning, as have most of the other stands; the contractors are already starting their task of demolition. The cases that took so long to fill and pack are stowed away, mostly empty, in the minivan. A delegate's cardigan found in one of the bedrooms and a mackintosh in the cloakroom – we take them with us, hoping their owners will claim them. I make a quick round of thank-yous – the conference manager and his deputy, the catering manager, the head porter and his staff. Everyone very friendly and relaxed and a little absentminded – we are already part of their past. Our whole year's work also – over in a few days.

CHAPTER 11

Postlude

'Once it's started it's over!'

I hope you will have experienced, in the smoothness of your
arrangements, how your long planning, work and foresight
have borne fruit in the few hours or days of your event. And now
your thoughts will turn first to the thank-yous – to the speakers
(not forgetting their fees, if promised, and travel or other
expenses, which you must chase after if they haven't already
submitted them); to chairs and committees; to hosts or benefactors; to all those whose effort and efficiency have contributed
to your success. Soon the bills will come in: check against the
estimates and the goods and services received and pay as you
can. Only now can you assess your profit and loss.

Post mortem

You may be making another assessment: how successful was
your conference in terms of the quality of the programme, the
suitability of the arrangements, the satisfaction of delegates, the
achievement of whatever object you had in view? Obviously
you will discuss this with your colleagues and committee, but
you may have decided to explore this more thoroughly by
undertaking a small market-research exercise. This will involve
preparing a questionnaire which you will ask your delegates to
complete, giving their comments on the conference. The time to
issue this, I suggest, is with the conference documents handed
out on arrival, with a plea for its return to you either on
departure or very shortly after the conference, by post. A good
deal of skill can go into the compilation of such documents, but
in order to quantify the responses it is essential to draft the
questions so that they can be answered very simply, in one
word – Yes or No; by ticking a box grading approval – Good,

Very Good, Moderate, Poor; to discover preferences, offer alternatives, one of which is to be ticked. Such questionnaires are completed anonymously, in theory ensuring that they express the truth. You may well develop a feeling about who they come from. Such post mortems, in my view, have only a limited value. In the first place, only a minority of delegates is likely to return them and those that do, in my experience, are generally those most inclined to find fault. A predominantly good assessment is a real cause for congratulation; a poor one must give you pause for thought. But you will certainly be thinking hard anyway of what shortcomings there were and how they could be rectified next time.

Conference proceedings

When it comes to publishing the proceedings of your conference, there are a number of options, which should have been looked at during the initial planning phase. It may be your normal practice to publish in your own journal – in fact the journals of many learned societies consist entirely of the proceedings of meetings and conferences held by them. This ensures circulation to your whole membership and all subscribers and enhances your journal contents without bringing in any extra revenue. If you do not have a journal or publishing expertise of your own, you may be able to sell the idea to the journal of another society (which will not produce revenue, but could be very good publicity for your conference, particularly if you see it as one of a series), or to a commercial publisher for a fee. If you have enough material, inevitably you will think of a book. This is an altogether more ambitious project and it is really a publishing decision whether to incur costs on such a scale: in addition to your delegates, will there be enough purchasers to cover such an outlay? If the topic is seen as a 'hot property' you may be approached by a publisher with an offer to take on the publication – and of course the ensuing profits – for a down payment or some degree of sponsorship of the conference. This could be a satisfactory solution if you have no publishing facilities yourself, but if you are a publisher and fairly confident of the financial basis of your conference, you should look at the figures very carefully before abandoning your right to publish.

Whatever is decided must be conveyed to the speakers from the outset, in your letter of invitation, when you will ask for texts of the papers and permission to reproduce them in the proceedings. If the publication is seen as a commercial venture, there is an argument for speakers participating in this, with a cut in the royalties or a down payment for the copyright, and this will mean individual contracts with the speakers. You should also consider a fee for the editor. At this early stage, too, you will have to decide how to handle the papers and whether the aim is to have the proceedings available at the conference itself. If this is your intention, the only practicable option is to ask your speakers for camera-ready copy, providing them with layouts and specifications which they must follow and, of course, an early copy date. As you can imagine, such co-operation is not always very easily achieved even though, on the whole and in principle, speakers are generally very happy to be published. The alternative – particularly if you aim to report the discussions and any conclusions reached – is to collect the papers at or immediately after the conference and to appoint an editor. In this case, you would re-set the papers and a good editor might produce a much better and more homogeneous work. But its appearance could, alas, be a good deal delayed and, if topicality is of the essence, camera-ready copy has to be your choice.

On the subject of costs there is, I know, an idea that the proceedings can provide a big boost to the conference finances, but this cannot be taken for granted and depends on whether the book is saleable to a large public besides your delegates. In fact, some conferences subsidise their proceedings by making the delegate's fee for the conference cover a copy of the proceedings, which by increasing the print number reduces the unit price of the volume.

You are not alone
Where to turn for help, when you seem to have exhausted all that books, guides, manuals, specimen letters and checklists can tell you? Nothing can replace a fellow conference organiser with experience that supplements your own. There is now a professional association for conference organisers, ACE International (the Association of Conference Executives), with a

membership that includes buyers (organisers like yourself) and sellers – hotels, travel agents, the suppliers of services. If organising conferences is your main activity, it would be worth joining ACE. Their journal, *Conference World* (though it seems mainly concerned with incentive conferences and product launches, where the glamour and money lie) will keep you *au fait* with the latest developments in the industry. Membership also brings you the invaluable *Conference Bluebook* (a Spectrum Group publication), with exhaustive lists of conference locations in the British Isles, and also ACE's own *Buyers' Guide* for conference and meeting planners: the suppliers and services listed here are all ACE members – not by any means all that exist, but quite a lot to go on with. From time to time, ACE organises seminars on various aspects of conference organising. If you have time for and can afford their mainly social meetings, you will meet other organisers as well as probably rather more suppliers. Incidentally, you will also have a chance to see some of the places where meetings of your own might be held.

I haven't talked about two particular services listed in the ACE *Buyers' Guide* because they are almost synonymous with conference organising. I have never used a conference placement agency to find accommodation for a conference, but I think there are occasions when such a service would be very well justified. If you are looking for accommodation in a place quite unfamiliar to you – perhaps a long way off or even abroad, where you do not have local contacts or advice, I would strongly recommend approaching such an agency, whose expertise, incidentally, is offered free to organisers (the venues pay a broker's commission for the introduction of business). Everything, of course, depends on the quality of the agency, their probity and their knowledge, but inevitably they must be in a position to assess locations as no individual organiser can, and I'm sure that if their standards are maintained and their numbers increase, so will their use.

It would, of course, be possible to hand over the whole organisation of your conference to a professional conference organiser, probably a company. For a large organisation that is not normally concerned with conference production embarking on a really large event, this is probably the best and most cost-effective solution, provided the choice of organiser is right.

But it does not really concern us, in a book that is about doing it yourself. However, I do think that for non-professional organisers, taking time from their normal roles as, say, professors, research workers, solicitors or accountants to produce a conference, a little professional advice in areas that seem problematical (or that I haven't covered) would be very supportive. Such conference consultants do exist and even on a low budget their fees would be money well spent.

The conference – *c'est toi!*

As you read this last page you'll have realised what a varied and demanding job organising a conference is and how much depends on you. You may also have reached some conclusions about the qualities a conference organiser needs. I suppose administrative ability about sums them up – the power to make things happen, to manage people without bossiness, to be tough when necessary but also kind, an eye for detail, an instinct for disaster, flexibility, humour – and the bonus of good health. A conference is a highly complex operation, with many diverse elements not entirely under your control welded into an integrated whole, a whole that is, or should be, an important event for those who come. For them, the delegates, some of whom may have travelled far and spent a lot of money, and who may have particular expectations, there should be a sense of a unique occasion. The special quality of this occasion is created by you and the staff and helpers you've been able to inspire. It is expressed in the way events, formal and informal, are arranged, but even more in the atmosphere of general welcome and helpfulness, creating in delegates a conviction of their importance and evoking the reaction that is the conference organiser's one true reward: 'That was a conference – that was!'

Conference calendar: a checklist of what to do and when to do it

Week 1

Decide: theme, object, audience. Consider: (a) size, (b) financial level, (c) date and place, (d) duration, (e) residential/non-residential.

Week 2

Decide in principle (a) – (e) above.

Week 3

Develop ideas for programme: treatment, format, speakers. Consider: exhibition, publication of proceedings.

Week 4

Draft first outline of programme. Decide on publication of proceedings. Investigate accommodation.

Week 5

Consider: visits or extracurricular activities, social programme.

Week 6

Compare facilities and estimates for accommodation. Draw up trial budget.

Week 7

Decide on and book accommodation. Confirm date. Invite speakers and chairs. Preliminary announcement in conference listings and press.

Week 8

Draft flyer or call for papers. Decide to hold exhibition.

Week 9

Approach exhibition builders for comparative tenders. Approach hosts of visits or extracurricular activities.

Week 10

Print flyer or call for papers. Inaugurate and cost social programme.

Week 11

Work on mailing list.

Week 12

Inspect site with chosen exhibition contractor. Continue negotiating details with location.

Week 13

Address envelopes or labels.

Week 14

Distribute flyer or call for papers. Preliminary write-up in selected press.

Week 15

Agree lay-out and costs for exhibition. Draft exhibition prospectus and prepare artwork.

Week 16

Calculate exhibition budget and decide charge for space.

Week 17

Approach coach operator for transport needs.

Week 18

Exhibition prospectus and artwork to printer.

Week 19

Finalise visits or extracurricular programme.

Week 20

Assess submitted papers, communicate with authors. Revise budget in light of visits and social programme.

Week 21

Negotiate concessionary fare for rail travellers, any other travel concession or package.

Week 22

Draft copy for programme and registration form.

Week 23

Finalise budget, decide conference fee.

Week 24

To printer: programme and registration form.

Week 25

Revise and extend mailing list.

Week 26

Prepare for programme distribution.

Week 27

—

Week 28
> Distribute programme and registration form. Press release. Press advertising.

Week 29
> Distribute exhibition prospectus. Mail programme to conference centre, hosts for visits, coach operator.

Week 30
> Write to speakers and chairs with programme and briefing for sessions. Bookings should begin.

Week 31
> —

Week 32
> Apply to national telecommunications authority for telephone facilities.

Week 33
> —

Week 34
> —

Week 35
> Draft programme handbook. Descriptive notes from exhibitors due. Speakers' abstracts and biographies due.

Week 36
> —

Week 37
> To printer: copy for programme handbook.

Week 38
> —

Week 39
> Checking visit to conference centre.

Week 40
> Proofs of handbook from printer. Follow-up distribution of programme if bookings need boost.

Week 41
> Return handbook proofs to printer with print number.

Week 42
> Order badges, conference packs. To printer: copy for invitations, tickets, menus.

Week 43
> Material for preprints due.

Week 44
Reproduce and collate preprints.

Week 45
Invitations, tickets, menus from printer. Prepare notices, directional signs, speakers' and chairs' display labels.

Week 46
Programme handbook (with exhibition handbook) from printer. Prepare and reproduce joining instructions for delegates and exhibitors.

Week 47
Prepare and reproduce attendance list. Address envelopes to delegates. Final advertisements in press.

Week 48
Documents and joining instructions to delegates, exhibitors and speakers.

Week 49
Visits lists with handbook to hosts. Transport brief with handbook to coach operator. Prepare delegates' and exhibitors' badges.

Week 50
Prepare briefs for location. Discuss staff brief with colleagues, agree and reproduce. Arrange staff bureau.

Week 51
To conference centre: handbook, numbers, rooming list, catering brief, brief for projectionist. Complete badges.

Week 52
Prepare and produce amendments to programme, final attendance list. To location: final number. Make packing list. Pack. Collect badges and material for conference packs, alphabetise, pack. Brief and all papers to staff.

APPENDIX 2

Sources of information

ACE International (the Association of Conference Executives), Riverside House, High Street, Huntingdon, Cambridgeshire PE18 6SG. Tel. 0480 57595.

Publications free to members include:

Conference & Meeting Planners Buyers' Guide. Wide range of conference services, including conference accommodation in centres and hotels, conference consultants and advisory services, interpreters, organising services, placement agencies, hotel booking services, etc. A limited number of copies are on sale to non-members at £5.00. Annual.

Conference World. Bi-monthly magazine for conference organisers.

Conference Help (annual).

Meetings – Finding Somewhere Different (annual).

Services:

ACE Executive Recruitment.

ACE-Plan Insurance. See Expo-Sure under 'Conference services' below. Special rates for members.

Conference accommodation – United Kingdom

British Association of Conference Towns, International House, 36 Dudley Road, Royal Tunbridge Wells, Kent TN1 1LB. Tel. 0892 33442.

British Universities Accomodation Consortium (BUAC), Box 273, University Park, Nottingham NG7 2RD. Tel. 0602 504571.

The Conference Blue Book, Spectrum Communications Ltd, Spectrum House, 191 The Vale, London W3 7 QS. Tel. 01 740 4444. Annual.

Conference Welcome: a Directory, Domino Books Ltd, Homeric House, Mount Pleasant, Douglas, Isle of Man. Tel. 0624 27130. Annual.

London Visitor & Convention Bureau, 26 Grosvenor Gardens, London SW1W 0DU. Tel. 01 730 3450.
Publishes *Convention London* (annual).

Conference accommodation – overseas

European Federation of Conference Towns, UK representative: Geoffrey Smith, 137 Sheen Road, Richmond, Surrey TW9 1YJ. Tel. 01 940 3431.

National Tourist Offices in countries concerned.

Conference services

Educational Foundation for Visual Aids (EFVA), The National Audio-Visual Aids Centre, The George Building, Normal College, Holyhead Road, Bangor, Gwynedd LL57 2PZ. Tel. 0248 370144.

Exhibitors' Handbook, Kogan Page Ltd, 120 Pentonville Road, London N1 9JN. Tel. 01 278 0433. Annual.

Expo-Sure Ltd, The Pantiles House, 2 Nevill Street, Royal Tunbridge Wells, Kent TN2 5SA. Tel. 0892 511500.
ACE International's recommended insurance agent, open to non-members.

Meeting Planners International, UK representative: Geoffrey Smith, 137 Sheen Road, Richmond, Surrey TW9 1YJ. Tel. 01 940 3431.

Regional offices of the National Trust.
For possible visits.

Regional tourist boards.
For places of interest, accommodation, catering and other facilities.

School Visits, Tours, Outings and Holidays – a Guide, Domino Books Ltd, Homeric House, Mount Pleasant, Douglas, Isle of Man. Tel. 0624 27130. Annual.
Ideas for tours and extracurricular activities.

The White Book: the International Production Directory to the Entertainment, Leisure, Conference and Exhibition Industries, Birdhurst Ltd, Unit 18, Central Trading Estate, Staines, Middlesex TW18 4XE. Tel. 0784 64441. Annual.
Includes sections on the conference and exhibition industry; transportation, travel and accommodation; television, radio and press; locations; professional services.

Other information sources, mainly for publicity

Benn's Media Directory, Benn Business Information Services Ltd, PO Box 20, Sovereign Way, Tonbridge, Kent TN9 1RQ. Tel. 0732 362666. Annual.

Commonwealth Universities Year Book, Association of Commonwealth Universities, John Foster House, 36 Gordon Square, London WC1H 0PF. Tel. 01 387 8572. Annual.

Direct Mail Data Book, Gower Publishing Co. Ltd, Gower House, Croft Road, Aldershot, Hampshire GU11 3HR. Tel. 0252 331551.

Forthcoming International Scientific and Technical Conferences, Aslib, 26 – 27 Boswell Street, London WC1N 3JZ. Tel. 01 430 2671. Quarterly.

A Guide to Effective Direct Mail, The Post Office, Royal Mail Marketing, 33 Grosvenor Place, London SW1X 1PX. Tel. 01 245 7031.

The Presentation of Information, Elizabeth Orna and Graham Stevens, Aslib, 26 – 27 Boswell Street, London WC1N 3JZ. Tel. 01 430 2671. To be published.

Whitaker's Almanack, J. Whitaker & Sons Ltd, 12 Dyott Street, London WC1A 1DF. Tel. 01 836 8911. Annual.

Willings Press Guide, Thomas Skinner Directories, Windsor Court, East Grinstead House, East Grinstead, West Sussex RH19 1XE. Tel. 0342 26972. Annual.

Checklist of main programme contents

Title page	Conference logo
	Organisation name
	Title of conference
	Date
	Place
	Descriptive paragraph
	Sponsors
	Organising committee
Main text	List of speakers and chairs
	Timetable
Practical information	Location
	Accommodation (sessions/catering/residence)
	Travel, hotel information
	Exhibition
	Social events
	Visits
Fees	
Registration form	

Registration form

REGISTRATION FORM

Name, place and date of conference

Application to attend   Closing date:

To:

Name . . . . First Name . . . . Title . . . .
Degrees . . . . Position . . . .
Organisation . . . .
Address . . . .
. . . . Postcode . . . . . Tel No . . . .
Invoice address if different from above . . . .
. . . .
. . . . Postcode . . . . . Tel No . . . .
I wish to register for the following:

>   *Conference resident   £000
>   *Conference non-resident   £000
>   (I will make my own accommodation arrangements)
>
>   Prices inclusive / exclusive of VAT [if applicable]
>
>   *delete as inapplicable

SPECIAL DIETARY OR OTHER REQUIREMENTS

Please specify

TRAVEL / WORKSHOPS / VISITS

I will travel by air* / car* / rail*

I would like to participate in the following:

Workshop 1 . . . . 2 . . . . 3 . . . . (please tick one)
Visit 1 . . . . 2 . . . . 3 . . . . 4 . . . . (please tick one)

Places on workshops and visits will be allocated on a first come, first served basis.

*delete as inapplicable

SOCIAL

I would like to attend: Civic Reception . . . . (please tick)
Conference Banquet . . . . (please tick)

---

*Please send an invoice

*I enclose a cheque for £

Cheques should be made payable to

*Please charge my Access   American Express

Visa   (please tick)   Account No.

with the sum of £

*delete as inapplicable

PLEASE NOTE: Applications mailed after the closing date MUST be accompanied by a cheque for the whole conference fee.

CANCELLATION: In the event of cancellation there will be a charge of £00 plus VAT. NO refund of the conference fee will be made to those cancelling after . . . .

Cheque Invoice No	Ack	Banquet	Travel	Paid	Docs

APPENDIX 5

Placing of screen and distance from audience

How high should the room be?

Many conference rooms have ceilings that are too low. This makes them very claustrophobic. Some rooms are not high enough to accommodate a screen big enough for every delegate to see properly. Use the simple criteria on this page to make sure your room and screen heights are sufficient. Note: the projected image must fill the screen.

Level of ceiling *or* bottom of lowest hanging height

$$S = \frac{D}{8}$$

Bottom of screen minimum of 4ft from ground

No person should be closer to screen than 2×5

$$H = \frac{D}{8} + 4$$

D

All dimensions should be worked in feet

H = Required height from floor level
D = Distance from screen position to position of rear seat
S = Screen height

118

Room arrangement

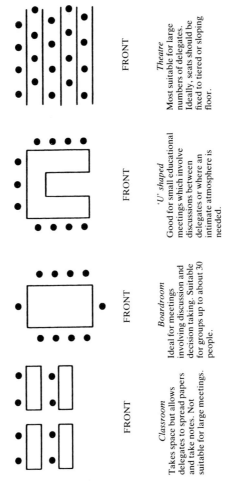

FRONT

Theatre
Most suitable for large numbers of delegates. Ideally, seats should be fixed to tiered or sloping floor.

FRONT

'U' shaped
Good for small educational meetings which involve discussions between delegates or where an intimate atmosphere is needed.

FRONT

Boardroom
Ideal for meetings involving discussion and decision taking. Suitable for groups up to about 30 people.

FRONT

Classroom
Takes space but allows delegates to spread papers and take notes. Not suitable for large meetings.

Platform arrangement

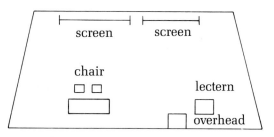

1. Slide plus overhead projection

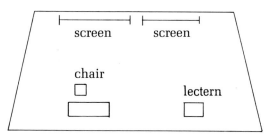

2. Two-screen slide presentation

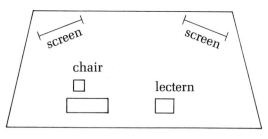

3. Angled screens

Notes for speakers and chairs and letter to go with programme

Name
Address

Dear

Name, place and date of conference

I can now send you a copy of the programme of this conference, in which you have kindly promised to take part. From it you will see how our project has developed and where your own contribution is placed.

As you know, the proceedings of the conference will be published and details of copy dates, layout instructions, etc., are enclosed herewith. / I hope you can let me have a text for preprinting not later than (a date ten weeks before the conference). / I hope you can let me have your text at or immediately after the conference.

I also enclose some notes for speakers and chairs, telling you a little more about how we hope to organise the sessions, the facilities available and the various arrangements we are making for your stay. It would be very helpful if you could complete and return the form which accompanies these notes as soon as is convenient.

Thank you in advance for helping us in this way and even more for your participation in our conference.

NOTES FOR SPEAKERS AND CHAIRS

<u>Name, place and date of conference</u>
Name . . . .

Your contribution is placed in session . . . . in the . . . .
of . . . . You have undertaken to talk about . . . .
. . . . and we hope for a paper of . . . .
minutes duration. We would like that period to allow some time
for discussion; *as we are preprinting your paper you may prefer
to speak to the highlights of the paper, giving delegates a chance
to question you about the full text.

The lecture theatre at . . . . seats 300, which we visualise as
about the size of audience we can expect. It can provide the usual
audiovisual facilities, overhead and 5cm × 5cm slide projector,
16mm projector, flipchart, etc.

You will be our guest at . . . . for the duration of the
conference and we are meeting travelling expenses (tourist class
airfare, second class rail).

To enable us to make suitable arrangements for your stay and
presentation and to complete the programme handbook, please
will you complete and return the questionnaire that follows these
notes.

*Omit if this does not apply

<u>Conduct of sessions</u>

1. Speakers

Speakers have been invited to speak for the specified times set out
in their letters of invitation and it is important not to overrun the
time allocated in the timed programme. Speakers will be
introduced by the chairs and at the end of papers some minutes
will be allowed for discussion. In dealing with questions,
speakers should answer as fully but as concisely as possible.

2. Discussion

It is hoped that as many people as possible will take part in the
discussion. They will be asked to give their names and affiliations
before speaking, to use the floor microphones if these are
provided and to keep their questions brief.

3. Chairs

The chair has the task of introducing speakers, giving the salient facts about the speakers' backgrounds and indicating their qualifications for speaking on the chosen topic in a two to three-minute introduction. He or she is responsible for ensuring that speakers do not overrun their allotted time and for managing discussion periods. For clarity's sake, it is often advisable to repeat the questions from the floor. In winding up the sessions, he or she should try to summarise briefly the main points emerging from the discussion and thank the speakers for their contributions.

Visual aids

1. Type

There is now a very wide choice of visual aids, but the two kinds most commonly used are still the overhead projector and the slide projector. Speakers should inform the conference secretary as soon as possible if they wish to use either of these devices. The following notes are a basic guide to these simple aids. Speakers who wish to make use of some of the more sophisticated technology available should discuss their presentation in detail with the conference secretary.

2. Purpose

The purpose of using visual aids is to communicate information more effectively than is possible by speech alone. To achieve this purpose they must be selected and prepared with some care.

3. Selection

(a) The lecture should not have too many slides or transparencies and each should illustrate a specific point.
(b) The information content of each should be restricted to what the audience can assimilate in a short space of time.
(c) Line drawings should be as simple as possible.
(d) Graphs are more easily assimilated than numerical data.
(e) Essential information should be conveyed by keywords, the detail being filled in verbally by the speaker.

4. Preparation

(a) Slides
The standard slide is 5cm × 5cm with an image area of 23mm × 35mm in which the longer dimension can be either horizontal or vertical. Dimensions of the originals should be in the ratio of 2:3.

The actual dimensions of the originals should not exceed 28cm × 40cm (11 × 16 in.).

Lettering should be set in capitals and lower case in an easy-to-read typeface, e.g. sans-serif. To be readable by an audience, the height of a capital letter should not be less than 1/50 of the height of the whole image, which means that if the original is prepared on a normal typewriter it should not exceed 130mm × 190mm (5 × 7½ in) overall.

Graphs and drawings can be prepared on sectional ruled paper provided the rules are pale blue (preferably) or pale green, but not orange, red or sepia. The drawing should be in black ink and on an A4 sheet (210mm × 297 mm), major lines should not be less than 0.8mm thick and secondary lines not less than 0.4mm thick.

Colour is useful in certain circumstances but does not show detail as clearly as monochrome and, during projection, requires almost total darkness in the auditorium.

Slides should be numbered and given to the projectionist in the order in which they are to be projected. In most locations the speaker's instructions to change slides are relayed verbally to the projectionist through the public address system, although push-button signals are sometimes provided.

(b) Transparencies
Overhead projectors are available in most locations, although not all of these provide really suitable conditions for viewing. The main problem is to get sufficient distance between the projector and the screen to get a large enough image on the screen.

On most projectors the usable transparency is 250mm × 250mm, which means that normally the height of an individual letter on a transparency should be between 5mm and 10mm if the image is to be readable over the whole auditorium.

Transparencies can be prepared manually, using felt-tip pens, or photographically, and the criteria for good slide making are also applicable to transparencies (see above).

INFORMATION SHEET

For return to conference secretary as soon as possible and not later than . . . . Type-written or capital letters, please.

Personal details

Name . . . . .Title . . . .
(As you wish it to appear in programme, attendance list and badge)
Degrees, etc. . . . .
Organisation . . . .
Address . . . .
. . . . Telephone number . . . .
Address for last 4 weeks before conference if different from
above . . . .
. . . .

Accommodation and travel

I shall need accommodation for the nights of . . . .
I expect to attend the conference banquet. civic
reception . . . . (please tick)
I expect to travel by air* / rail* / car*
*delete as inapplicable

Projection requirements

I shall need the following: overhead projector
5cm × 5cm slide projector
16mm film projector
flipchart
Other (please specify)

Biographical note (up to 150 words)

Your paper

Your revised thoughts on title, if different from that shown in
programme . . . .

Abstract (up to 150 words)

Catering brief

CATERING BRIEF

To: The Catering Manager

<u>Day 1</u>

from 16.00	Registration of delegates Tea and coffee	foyer
18.00	Bar open	main bar
19.00	Dinner	dining room
20.30	Drinks reception	main lounge
up to 24.00	Bar open (special extension)	main bar

<u>Day 2</u>

from 08.00	Breakfast	dining room
10.45	Coffee	foyer adjoining auditorium
12.00	Bar open	main bar
13.00	Lunch	dining room
15.30	Tea	foyer adjoining auditorium
18.00	Bar open	main bar
19.00	Dinner	dining-room
up to 24.00	Bar open (special extension)	main bar and lounge bar

<u>Day 3</u>

from 08.00	Breakfast	dining-room
10.45	Coffee	foyer adjoining auditorium

12.00	Bar open	main bar
13.00	Lunch	dining room
15.45	Tea	foyer adjoining auditorium
18.00	Bar open	main bar
19.00	Director's party	VIP bar
19.00	Pre-Banquet reception	main lounge
20.00	Banquet	dining-room
21.30 to 24.00	Bar open (special extension)	lounge bar
21.30 to 24.00	Disco Bar open (special extension)	main bar

Day 4

| from 08.00 | Breakfast (Conference disperses) | dining room |

A formula for giving figures of bed nights and meals

(Many locations have their own standard form that they will ask you to complete)

	Bed night	Breakfast	Coffee	Lunch	Tea	Dinner	Reception	Banquet
Day 1					49	49	49	
Day 1/2	49							
Day 2		49	55	55	55	50		
Day 2/3	50							
Day 3		50	55	55	55			59
Day 3/4	50							
Day 4		50						
Totals:	149	149	110	110	159	99	49	59

Notice that the numbers throughout the conference are not constant. You may have a few non-resident delegates – hence the higher numbers for coffee, lunch and tea. There are likely to be guests at the banquet, offsetting the odd delegate who does not attend. One of your delegates only arrives in time for morning coffee on Day 2.

Projection brief

PROJECTION BRIEF

To: The Projection Department

Day 1

08.45	Main auditorium Speakers' meeting	projectionist PA system throughout
09.00	Session 1 Chair's opening remarks	
09.15	Paper 1 Dr A	5cm × 5cm slide projector
10.00	Paper 2 Dr B	overhead projector
10.40	Coffee	
11.20	Paper 3 Dr C	5cm × 5cm slide projector overhead projector
11.50	Paper 4 Dr D	overhead projector
12.30	Discussion	roving microphones
13.00	Lunch	
14.30	Parallel Sessions	

	Main auditorium	projectionist PA system throughout	Lecture theatre B	projectionist
	Session 2a		Session 2b	
14.30	Paper 5 Dr E	5cm × 5cm slide projector	Paper 5b Dr F	overhead
15.15	Paper 6 Dr G	16mm film overhead	Paper 6b Dr H	5cm × 5cm slide projector

16.00	Tea	
16.30	Main auditorium Session 3	projectionist PA system throughout
	Paper 7 Dr I	5cm × 5cm slide projector overhead projector
17.15	Discussion	roving microphones

Continue with the same formula for each of the sessions on subsequent days. The detailed instructions avoid confusion and any suggestion that your requirements were not stated clearly.

Letter of invitation to speakers

Name
Address

Dear

Intelligent Retrieval: a conference

place and date

This conference will examine the state of the art in experimental retrieval systems and will explore possibilities for the future. The programme will consider unsolved problems in automatic intelligence, automatic textual analysis, natural language processing, expert systems, fifth-generation computer architecture and intelligent database management systems. As it will be examining activity at the frontiers of computer science, we believe such a conference should be relevant to those seeking to improve the design and performance of retrieval systems and should draw a large audience of academics, data processing professionals and information specialists.

I am writing now on behalf of the organising committee / - and on the suggestion of . . . . -/ in the hope I can persuade you to be one of our speakers.

The attached information sheet tells you a little more about the project, with some initial thoughts on the programme and how we plan to develop our theme; and I am inviting you to address the conference in the session on . . . . in the morning/ afternoon of . . . . talking about . . . . I have in mind a paper of . . . . minutes duration, which we hope will be followed by a discussion period in which you would take a leading part.

You would, of course, be our guest at . . . . for the duration of the conference and your travel expenses would be met. / We do also have in mind an honorarium of . . . . which I hope would be acceptable to you.

The proceedings of the conference will be published and for this we shall need your text at or very shortly after the conference / camera-ready copy (layout details and sheets for typing the text will be provided) not later than . . . . , as we plan to make the proceedings available to delegates at the start of the conference.

I do very much hope you will be able to accept our invitation to take part in what I believe will be an exciting and important programme. If you can accept, I will look forward to having further discussions about your contribution in due course. Meanwhile, you would be adding to your kindness if you would reply with your decision as soon as possible. I eagerly look forward to hearing from you.

Acknowledgement of registration

Name
Address

Dear

Name, place and date of conference

Thank you for your application to attend this conference.

Receipt of your payment for the sum of £ . . . . . in respect of the conference fee is acknowledged with thanks. / An invoice for the conference fee is enclosed.

Receipt of this payment will be regarded as confirmation of your attendance and to secure your place it is important that all fees should be paid not later than. . . .

Shortly before the conference a copy of the conference and exhibition handbook will be sent to you together with relevant information about accommodation and other arrangements at [conference location].

Enclosed is a leaflet giving details of conference discount rail fares [if applicable].

Joining instructions for delegates

JOINING INSTRUCTIONS

(Name of delegate) . . . .

Name, place and date of conference

Your conference documents are enclosed.

Accommodation

*Accommodation has been reserved for you for the nights of Monday, Tuesday, Wednesday (date) in . . . .

*You are attending as a non-resident

You will*/will not* attend the banquet on Wednesday.

If you have not informed the conference organiser of any special requirements – diet, position of room, personal handicap – please do so immediately.

Catering

All meals during the conference will be taken in the dining room. Coffee and tea will be served between sessions in the foyer adjoining the lecture theatre, where the exhibition and reception desk are also located. On Monday, dinner will be served from 19.00 hours.

Registration

Registration will start at 17.00 hours on Monday, in the foyer of the residence*/hotel* where you are staying. On registration, you will be given a room key (which it is important to return on departure) and will be directed to your room. You are asked to vacate your room before noon on the day of departure.

Travel

Buses will meet trains arriving at . . . . . . railway station between 17.00 and 19.00 hours on Monday, to convey delegates to the conference centre. At the conclusion of the conference, on Thursday, buses will depart from the centre for . . . . station at 14.00 hours.

Social programme

All delegates are invited to a 'welcome' reception, on the site of the exhibition, from 20.45 hours on Monday.

Buses for the civic reception will depart from the main entrance to the centre at 20.00 hours on Tuesday.

The conference banquet, at 19.30 for 20.00 hours on Wednesday, will be held in the dining room.

Workshops

Places have been allocated in order of application. See handbook for times and places. Lists will be displayed on the noticeboard.

Visits

Places have been allocated in order of application, taking second choices into account. Attendance lists for visits will be displayed on the noticeboard. Visits buses will depart from the main entrance at 14.15 hours on Wednesday and return to the same place.

Telephone

The telephone number of the conference reception will be . . . . Messages for delegates can be taken on this number during office hours and will be conveyed to them at the first opportunity. Call-boxes for outgoing calls are available throughout the centre.

Dress

Dress for the conference will be informal.

Supplement to programme and final attendance list

These will be available for delegates on registration.

Cancellations / changes / queries

Please contact the conference organiser, ..., without delay.

*for organiser to delete where inapplicable when completing individual forms.

Staff brief

STAFF BRIEF

To: Members of staff DG (Director)   From: AB (Conference
                       CD   Organiser)
                       EF
                       GH
                       IJ
                       KL

Previous day

from 10.00	Erection of exhibition at conference centre	Exhibition contractor
17.00	Depart for place of conference	AB
by 19.00	All conference material loaded for early departure	CD, EF
20.00	Arrive at conference centre – prepare notices for board	AB

Day 1

08.00	Transport with conference material departs	CD, EF, GH
08.00	At conference centre Breakfast Check registration arrangements with residence/hall porter	AB
10.00	Meet local conference manager, check lecture room(s), projection, layout	AB
	Check progress on exhibition erection	AB
	Meet catering manager	AB
12.00	Access to exhibition for exhibitors	

12.00	Transport with conference material arrives	CD, EF, GH
	Set up conference desk and office	AB, CD
	Set up exhibit	EF, GH
13.00	Lunch	AB, CD, EF, GH
14.00	Rest of staff arrive	IJ, KL
15.00	Set up reception desk, arrange badges, documents, lists	AB, CD, GH
15.30	Director arrives by car	DG
16.30	To railway station to meet buses	EF
17.00 – 19.00	Buses meet delegates and convey to centre	
	Usher delegates on board and control flow	EF
17.00 – 19.00	Registration	AB, CD, GH, IJ
19.00	Dinner	All
	(Reception desk staffed throughout, taking turns)	AB, CD, GH
20.00	Speakers and chairs meet projectionist at lecture theatre, check projection, etc.	DG, AB KL
20.30	Conference opening and keynote address in lecture theatre	All
21.30	Drinks reception in exhibition area	All
Day 2		
from 07.30	Breakfast	All
from 08.30	Reception desk open – staffed throughout	AB, CD
	Check on duties and arrangements	All
09.00	Speakers at lecture theatre for brief check	AB, KL
	Session 1 – lecture theatre	
	Rapporteurs and discussion aides	KL, EF
	On desk	AB, CD
10.30	Coffee break – exhibition area	All

11.00	Session 1 (cont.) Rapporteurs and discussion aides	GH, IJ
12.30	Bar open	
13.00	Lunch	All
14.15	Speakers at lecture theatre for brief check	AB, KL
14.30	Session 2 – lecture theatre Rapporteurs and discussion aides	KL, EF
15.45	Tea in exhibition area Desk staffed	All AB, CD
16.15	Session 2 (cont.) Rapporteurs and discussion aides	GH, IJ
16.40	President arrives at station – meet	DG
18.30	Dinner	All
19.30	Buses for civic reception – shepherd delegates on board	EF, GH, IJ
19.45	Buses depart for assembly rooms, president and party by car	DG, AB
20.00	Reception at assembly rooms	All
23.00	Buses for return to centre – shepherd delegates on board	All
Day 3 from 07.30	Breakfast	All
from 08.30	Reception desk open – staffed throughout Check on duties and arrangements	AB, CD All
09.00	Speakers at lecture theatre for brief check	AB, KL
09.15	Session 3 – lecture theatre Rapporteurs and discussion aides	KL, EF
10.30	Coffee break – exhibition area	All
11.00	Session 3 (cont.) Rapporteurs and discussion aides	GH, IJ
11.30	Briefing meeting for tour guides – conference office	AB, tour guides

12.30	Bar open	
13.00	Lunch	All
14.00 for 14.15	Despatch visits buses – main entrance	AB, EF
14.15	Check projection for workshops – projectionist	KL
14.30	Workshops (4)	KL, IJ, to monitor
15.00	Agree top table plan with director Brief president for thanks in banquet speech	DG, AB, President
	Type place cards and table plan	CD
15.45	Tea	All
16.15	Workshops continue	KL, IJ
18.30	Set out top table place cards	AB
19.00	Meet toastmaster	AB
19.30	Director's and president's party for top table (small anteroom)	DG, KL, AB
19.30	Delegates' reception – main foyer	All
20.00	Banquet	All
22.00	Disco	All

Day 4

from 07.30	Breakfast	All
from 08.30	Reception desk open – staffed throughout	AB, CD
	Check on duties and arrangements	All
	Notices re departure on board	AB
09.15	Speakers at lecture theatre for brief check	KL, EF
09.30	Session 4 – lecture theatre	
	Rapporteurs, discussion aids	KL, IJ
	Dismantle exhibit	GH, EF
10.45	Coffee	All
11.15	Final session – lecture theatre President in chair	DG, KL
	Closing address and thanks	

12.00	Exhibition contractor to dismantle stands	
12.30	Bar open	
12.45	Lunch	All
from 13.45	Buses for railway station – shepherd delegates on board	KL, IJ, EF
14.00	Director leaves by car, taking president Pack and load transport	DG All
15.00	Transport leaves for home Thank-yous and goodbyes	CD, EF, GH AB
16.00	Homebound train	AB, IJ, KL

Checklist for 'keeping in touch'

Conference centre

Contract and/or exchange of letters setting out facilities hired and conditions and charges for the letting.

Written confirmation of any alterations or additions.

Conference programme announcement.

Programme/handbook giving place and time of registration, catering, sessions, social and all other events.

Catering brief with time and place of meals, coffee and tea breaks, bar opening, social events in which food or drink are involved (Appendix 9).

Projection brief stating what public address and projection facilities are needed, where and at what times a projectionist is required (Appendix 10).

Rooming list.

Catering numbers for each meal.

Speakers

Formal letter of invitation (Appendix 11).

Letter acknowledging agreement to speak.

Conference programme announcement with brief and notes for speakers (Appendix 8).

Final documents: personal letter, joining instructions (Appendix 13), handbook, expenses claim form, invitations, tickets, preprints (if issued), attendance list.

'Thank-you' letter.

Transport

Specification of transport needs to coach operator(s) for estimate.

Acceptance of estimate.

Conference programme announcement 'to remind'.

Conference handbook with schedule confirming final transport requirements, stating destinations, time and place for pick-up and return.

Labels with destinations for display in coaches.

Delegates

'Flyer' or call for papers.

Programme announcement with registration form (Appendix 4).

Letter acknowledging registration and sending invoice (Appendix 12).

Final documents: joining instructions (Appendix 13), handbook, attendance list, invitations, tickets, preprints (if issued).

On arrival: badges, programme supplement, final attendance list, maps.

Exhibitors

Prospectus (Appendix 18) with 'flyer' or programme announcement.

Confirmation of booking with invoice.

Final documents: as for delegates plus special note with plan of exhibition area, directions for access, erection of exhibit, details of special facilities and telephone (if requested).

Staff

Final documents and joining instructions as for delegates.

Staff brief (Appendix 14).

Miscellaneous

Directional signs.

Display labels for chairs and speakers in sessions.

Exhibition layouts

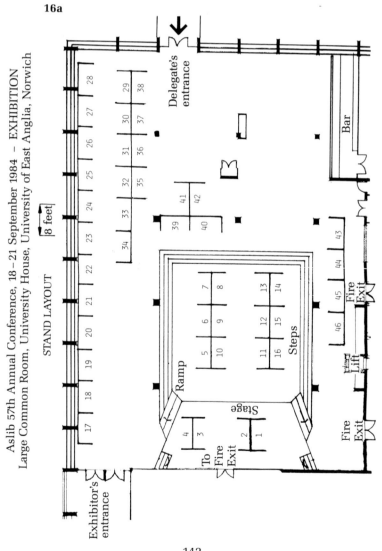

16a

Aslib 57th Annual Conference, 18 – 21 September 1984 – EXHIBITION
Large Common Room, University House, University of East Anglia, Norwich

STAND LAYOUT

16b

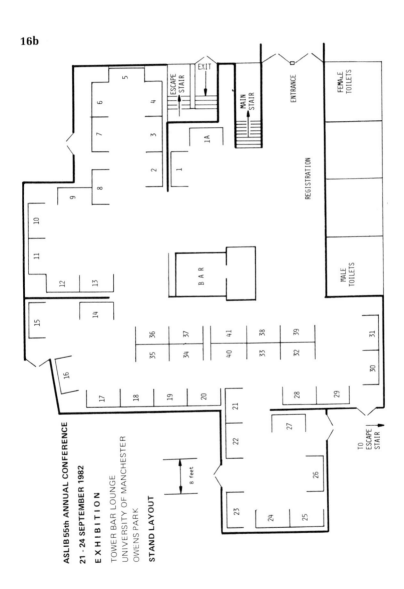

Sketch of basic stand

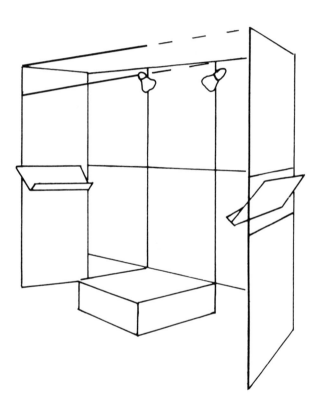

APPENDIX 18

Exhibition prospectus

The Association for Information Management

57th ANNUAL CONFERENCE

EXHIBITION

University of East Anglia, Norwich

18–21 September 1984

Space at the University of East Anglia (UEA) is not unlimited, so early application is strongly advised to ensure a place in this important exhibition. Located at the focal point of the conference, the exhibition will also be open to local library and information staff and interested members of the Norwich public, while the official opening at the Welcome Reception will give exhibitors and delegates a chance to meet each other in a leisurely and convivial way.

1. PLACE

Exhibition space is situated in the Large Common Room, University House, the focal point of the conference, where a bar and lounge are located and coffee and tea between sessions will be served.

2. ALLOTMENT OF SPACE

Space is offered in units of 8ft × 4ft, using panels which provide a back wall and side partitions, and the exhibitor's name is displayed in standard lettering across the front of the stand.

Equipment must fit within the area of space hired (see plan overleaf for disposition of the units).

3. TIME

The exhibition will open at 21.15 hours on Tuesday, 18 September, with a Welcome Reception for all delegates. It will continue from 09.15 – 17.30 hours on 19 and 20 September and from 09.15 to 13.00 on 21 September.

4. ACCESS

The Large Common Room will be open for the installation of exhibits from 10.00 hours on Tuesday, 18 September and all material must be removed by 15.00 hours on Friday, 21 September. Access to the Large Common Room is by the Buses Entrance.

5. COST

Space and facilities

A composite fee per 8ft × 4ft unit of £240 plus VAT at the current rate covers the hire of space, erection of the stand with the exhibitor's name displayed in standard lettering, one 100-watt spotlight with one individual 13-amp power point, one table (3ft × 2ft) and 2 chairs. Additional units will be charged at the same rate.

Hanging shelves for display can be hired at £8.00 + VAT per 4ft shelf and additional spotlights can also be hired at £8.00 + VAT per light. Special requirements for electrical power over and above lighting requirements (ie. power for VDUs, dedicated supplies etc.) must be notified on the booking form.

Photographic or display literature may be pinned or stuck to the panels.

Exhibitors' representatives

The hire charge for space includes the attendance of one exhibitor's representative per unit, who has access to the Aslib Conference sessions, morning coffee, afternoon tea and lunch on each day of the conference, and receptions, including the Conference Banquet. Additional representatives, with the same entitlement, will be charged £85.00 + VAT.

Accommodation can be booked for exhibitors' representatives in UEA Halls of Residence, where the delegates will be staying, at the price of £16.50 per night (dinner, bed and breakfast) plus VAT.

6. TELEPHONES

Exhibitors needing telephone facilities on their stand should apply direct to: British Telecom Norwich, ——

as soon as possible and not later than 29 June 1984.

The full cost of such installations must, of course, be borne by the exhibitor.

7. HANDBOOK

All exhibitors are invited to provide a short descriptive note of their exhibit of not more than 50 words for inclusion, free of charge, in the Conference Handbook. This should be submitted as soon as possible and cannot be included if it is not received by 15 June 1984.

Advertising space is available as follows:

Full page (180mm × 120mm) £70.00

8. CONDITIONS OF HIRE

i. Fifty per cent of the hire charge for space (£120.00 per unit) must be paid on application, the balance on receipt of invoice, which will accompany confirmation of the booking, and not later than 1 August 1984.

In the case of failure to pay by this date, the organiser reserves the right to regard the exhibitor as having withdrawn from the exhibition and to reallocate the space elsewhere. The deposit will remain the property of the organiser. In the event of cancellation, there will be no refund of the space hire charge.

ii. Advertisement space in the programme will be invoiced separately on publication.

iii. A representative of the exhibitor must be present and responsible for the exhibit for all the time that the exhibition is open.

iv. Exhibitors must comply with the terms of access for installation and dismantling as set out in paragraph 4 above and with the limitations on the type and size of the display equipment cited in paragraph 2. The use of sound reproducing equipment and loudspeakers is not permitted.

v. Units of 8ft × 4ft only can be let.

vi. Units must not be sub-let.

vii. The exhibitors exhibit entirely at their own risk. Aslib is not liable for any losses or damage to persons or property which the exhibitors or their agents may sustain. (Insurance against such contingencies is recommended.)

viii. Exhibitors may not alter the appointments of the exhibition area and any damage caused by the exhibitors or their agents to the fixtures or property must be made good at the exhibitors' expense. Exhibitors should also indemnify Aslib against liabilities, actions, costs, claims and compensation for injury or loss to any persons or damage to or loss of any property on their part. Exhibitors should be adequately insured against such liabilities.

9. APPLICATION FOR SPACE

Application for space should be made by completing the form herewith and returning it, accompanied by the deposit, as soon as possible (not later than 29 June 1984 if telephone facilities are required) to The Conferences Secretary, Professional Development Group, Aslib,——

ASLIB 57th ANNUAL CONFERENCE

EXHIBITION

University of East Anglia, Norwich

18 – 21 September 1984

To: The Conferences Secretary, Professional Development Group, Aslib, ——

Application for space
(please complete this form in block letters throughout)

Please reserve . . . . unit(s) (8ft × 4ft) at £240 per unit plus VAT in accordance with the conditions laid down.

Organisation . . . .
(Please show organisation as it should be printed for display on the stand)

Address . . . .
. . . .
. . . .

One 100-watt spotlight and one 13-amp power point are provided per unit

1. Do you need any additional power? Yes* / No*
   If Yes, please request . . . . 13-amp power point(s) @ £20 plus VAT each

   Please give details of loading & use . . . .
   . . . .

2. Do you need an additional spotlight? Yes* / No*
   If Yes, please request . . . . additional 100-watt spotlight(s) @ £8.00 plus VAT each

3. Do you require telephone facilities? Yes* / No*
   If Yes you should apply direct to: British Telecom Norwich,
   ___

4. Please supply . . . 4ft display shelves @ £8.00 plus VAT each

5. Name of contact (for invoice, etc)
   . . . .
   Telephone number . . . .

6. Name(s) of representative(s) at exhibition if different from above
   . . . .
   . . . .

7. Payment
   I enclose cheque for
      deposit (50% of total letting fee)* £ . . . .
      whole letting fee* £ . . . .
   Please send invoice for balance of fee* £ . . . .

   Payment should be made direct to Aslib immediately on receipt of invoice

(Space will be allocated in date order of receipt of application. All the locations are well placed from the point of view of accessibility to the public, but applicants may indicate, on the plan on the reverse of this form, their preference as regards position (giving a second and third choice), which will be adhered to if practicable).

*delete as inapplicable

Index

150